THE GREEK TYRANTS

THE GREEK TYRANTS

A. Andrewes
MBE, MA, FBA

*Wykeham Professor of Ancient History
in the University of Oxford*

**HUTCHINSON UNIVERSITY LIBRARY
LONDON**

Hutchinson & Co (Publishers) Ltd
3 Fitzroy Square, London W1

London Melbourne Sydney Auckland
Wellington Johannesburg and agencies
throughout the world

First published 1956
Reprinted 1958, 1960, 1962, 1964,
1966, 1969, 1971, 1974, and 1977
© A. Andrews 1974

Printed in Great Britain by litho at The Anchor Press Ltd
and bound by Wm Brendon & Son Ltd
both of Tiptree, Essex

ISBN 0 09 029564 1 (paper)

CONTENTS

PREFACE

As will be clear from every chapter of this book, the study of early Greek politics is hampered by lack of documentary detail of the kind which might illustrate the machinery of government and the structure of classes. The historian need not despair, provided he keeps in mind the nature of the gap in his evidence, but he is tempted to hedge his statements with "probably" and "possibly", and though I have tried to concentrate on material about which positive assertions can profitably be made, enough of these notes of doubt remain in my text.

Consistency in the transliteration of Greek names and words is almost impossible. No problem arises where there are specifically English forms like Athens or Aristotle: in general I have given names the latinized forms which may be more familiar (Alcaeus, not Alkaiòs), though with the representation of Greek *k* by *c* it is perhaps worth noting that those who have frequent occasion to name *e.g.* Cimon generally pronounce him Kimon rather than Simon: but I have not latinized Greek words, most of which will be unfamiliar in any case (so *hyperakrioi*, not *hyperacrii*), nor some of the more intractable names (there seems no gain in disguising Rhaikelos as Rhaecelus, which is nobody's pronunciation).

Since all dates are B.C., I have omitted these letters throughout.

I must emphasize my debt to two scholars untimely dead: Alan Blakeway's eager, even uproarious, teaching first introduced me to Greek history, and from his lectures on the seventh century these pages are (however remotely) descended; and the period covered here was the special field of his pupil and my contemporary, T. J. Dunbabin, whose laconic advice was always both steadying and stimulating. I thank Sir Maurice Bowra and Mr. R. Meiggs who read and discussed drafts of my text, Prof. D. L. Page for much conversation about Alcaeus, Prof. C. M. Robertson and Dr. P. Jacobsthal for archaeological first aid most generously given, though none of these are at all responsible for my errors; Mr. G. E. M. de Ste. Croix for reading proofs; and most of all Prof. H. T. Wade-Gery for wise and unstinted help at every stage.

6

CHAPTER I

THE BACKGROUND OF TYRANNY

TYRANNIES are to be found in all periods of Greek history, from the time when aristocratic government began to break down in the early seventh century, to the closing stages of Greek resistance to Rome in the second century. A tyrant was roughly what we should call a dictator, a man who obtained sole power in the state and held it in defiance of any constitution that had existed previously. This might be done by mere force for the sake of personal power, but the common justification of dictatorship, then as now, was the dictator's ability to provide more effective government. There are times when it can plausibly be asserted that the existing machinery of state is unable to cope with a crisis arising from external pressure or internal tension, and it was mainly at such times that support could be found in a Greek city for the strong rule of a single tyrant. Such occasions might also be manufactured, and even when the need was genuine the tyrant was likely to go beyond what was called for by the immediate crisis: personal ambition and public necessity cannot be neatly disentangled, nor is it ever easy for an autocrat to resign.

A tyrant, in these Greek terms, is not necessarily a wicked ruler, but he is an autocrat (and generally a usurper) who provides a strong executive. The traditionally wicked kings of English history, like John, are not the best examples of tyranny: a closer analogy would be given by Henry VII, whose powerful centralized government was acceptable because of the chaos of the Wars of the Roses. Cromwell and Napoleon and Mussolini were all clearly tyrants, not because their rule was good or bad, but because of the manner in which they assumed power and of the kind of break they made with the régimes under which they came to the front.

Some Greek tyrants were merely military figures, like Hippocrates of Gela in Sicily at the beginning of the fifth century. His successor Gelon, who conquered Syracuse, justified his rule by his defeat of the Carthaginian invasion of 480, and the rise of some other tyrants was connected with external pressure of this kind. In 405, during another Carthaginian invasion, Dionysius I gained control of Syracuse and held it till his death nearly forty years later; a powerful man, hard to assess because we have only his enemies' account of him, but specially important to us because he was a conspicuous figure in the world of Plato, with whom he quarrelled, and his career influenced the views of fourth-century philosophers on tyranny. Other tyrants were actually imposed by outside powers, like those set up by the Persians in the late sixth century to rule the East Greek cities under their control: others again were established in Greek cities as a direct or indirect result of the pressure exerted by the conflict of the great Hellenistic monarchies in the period after Alexander's death.

These various tyrannies are, in the main, incidental to the course of Greek history after the late sixth century, and hardly constitute a separate problem in themselves. The main concern of this book is with the earlier group which begins with the accession of Cypselus of Corinth about 650, and ends with the expulsion of the sons of Peisistratus from Athens in 510. When historians speak of "the age of the tyrants" in Greece, it is this period that they mean, a period when so many Greek cities underwent a tyranny that we naturally look for some general cause in the circumstances of the time. The causes are largely internal, to be found in the oppressiveness or inadequacy of the aristocracies which held power in the early seventh century. The tyrants mark a turning-point in the political development of Greece, the moment when an old order was breaking down and a new order was not yet established. It is this which makes them interesting as a group, coupled with the interest of the period itself and the quality of individual tyrants.

This is the time when the civilization of archaic Greece was in full flower. By 650 we have left Homer behind, and have reached the age of Archilochus and the early lyric poets, who speak with an intense and personal emotion of what they felt and did and suffered. A century of trade and exploration, from 750 to 650, had enlarged the geographical frontiers of Greek experience, discovering or rediscovering Egypt, Syria and the Black Sea in the East, Italy and Sicily in the West. The fruits of this are seen in the orientalizing styles of Greek pottery, and the finest of these early fabrics, the Protocorinthian, was produced at Corinth in the last generation of the Bacchiad aristocracy and at the beginning of Cypselus' tyranny. The tyrants, aristocrats themselves by birth, played their part in all this and were lavish patrons of poets and artists, and great builders of temples and public works. Many of them were also formidable in the world of politics, and Cypselus' son Periander made his influence felt far beyond the limits of Corinthian territory.

But historically we are still in the twilight. For the seventh century we have to fit together scattered pieces of evidence, to reconstruct history as well as to interpret. The following chapters make some attempt at narrative and are roughly in order, but they are nevertheless sections of an argument more than sections of a story, intended to clarify the various political, military and economic factors in the situation in which the tyrants appeared.

(a) GREEK MONARCHY

The first thing to be done is to consider the main lines of the political development into which the tyrants fit. At the beginnings of Greek history stand the kings of their various cities, shadowy figures for the most part. The prose authors who wrote about them, from the fifth century onwards, had little to go on except names, but they were unwilling to leave a historical vacuum, and gave the history of these early rulers in detail which was often quite obviously fictitious. We need not doubt the fact that monarchy was the normal constitution of the primitive Greek state, but the default of genuine tradition means that when we come to consider what kind of kings ruled in Greece, we can proceed only by inference, from the nature of their titles, from Homer, from later survivals or from analogy.

It has for instance been noted that all the ordinary Greek words for king appear to be of non-Greek origin, and it might be deduced from this that the more absolute style of monarchy was something originally foreign to the Greek mind, something that they found existing when they entered the Greek peninsula and in some sense took over from the pre-Greek inhabitants. However that may be, the notion of monarchy was established among them early, and the normal word for king (*basileus*) was firmly entrenched in Homer's language as the title for both Greek and oriental monarchs, for Agamemnon and Priam alike.

Agamemnon is an absolute king in the sense that he may act counter to the unanimous view of his followers, as in the opening scene of the *Iliad*, and if he summons an assembly, as he does in the second book, he is not bound to respect its wishes. When he repents of the wrong he has done to Achilles, it is not because he has been overborne by the other chiefs but because he himself realizes his fault, and even at this stage he still feels that Achilles should give way to him as the "more kingly". Yet the council of the Greek chiefs is obviously a normal and necessary institution, and the assembly of the army must have some standing, or why should it be summoned? In the *Odyssey* Ithaca is a political chaos while the king is away, a chaos which neither nobles nor people are able to resolve, to be ended only by Odysseus' return or Penelope's remarriage, or perhaps by the self-assertion of Telemachus suddenly grown up. The king is essential to the kingdom: he could not, and does not, manage without a council; the assembly exists in some sense and the kingdom would be incomplete without it, but it has not yet asserted power as against any other element. Precise constitutional definitions would be out of place here. This is how Homer thought the great kingdoms of the heroic past should be represented, and he gives us this indication of the way in which early Greeks thought about early monarchy[1].

For later survivals we look first to Sparta, where a double kingship, hereditary in two families, was an effective power till the late third century. An archaic Spartan document (*see* Chapter VI) uses the word *archagetai* for the kings, a purely Greek word meaning roughly "first leaders", applied elsewhere to the founders of colonies and sometimes the secondary title of a god: it sounds less absolute than "king", but it is hard to be sure that there is any essential difference. In classical times the Spartan king is referred to by the normal word *basileus*. His powers were extensive when he was in command of a military expedition (but the state decided if there was to be an expedition, and who was to command it), much more restricted at home, where he performed certain sacrifices and judged certain classes of lawsuit. It may be presumed that his competence was once wider in all three fields, military, religious and judicial, and a sign that he had lost some political power too is to be seen in the oath which was sworn every month between the kings and the ephors (the chief magistrates), in which the kings swore to observe the existing laws, while the ephors on behalf of the city swore to maintain the kings' position provided that they kept their oath. This one-sided bargain reflects an early limitation of the kings' autocratic powers. By classical times they were so much attenuated that Aristotle describes the Spartan kings as "hereditary generals"[2].

Elsewhere we find that the king survives, as at Athens, in the title of an annually elected official, hardly distinguishable from his brother magistrates except that he conducted the more ancient of the state sacrifices. Athenian tradition held that the other great magistracies had been created by taking away from the king certain of his spheres of competence, and tradition is surely here correct in principle[3]. A different kind of survival is found in Macedon, where a more primitive and autocratic monarchy was still in power in the fourth century, limited only by frequent civil war and by the rights of the assembled army, which confirmed the appointment of a king (de facto, the succession was roughly hereditary).

The executive in the developed Greek constitution descends from the power of the early kings, indeed the constitution may be thought of as a series of progressive limitations on the executive. In the primitive state, especially in a period of war and migration, it was necessary that the executive should be strong, and natural to leave it relatively unchecked. It was equally natural that the power of the king should be curtailed, as Greece settled down to a quieter and more civilized life, in which the rights of the individual aristocrat seemed more important than the need of the whole state for an effective executive.

(b) GREEK ARISTOCRACY

The transition from monarchy to aristocracy was no doubt often gradual, especially in those cities where the title of king survived later as the name of a magistracy. It is normally too far back in time for us to fix a precise date, and the stories told about the decline and fall of kingship are usually fiction. In some places, as at Corinth, it was believed that the last king had been deposed or killed. The successors to the kings were hereditary groups, as is shown by their patronymic names: the Eupatridae of Athens (the "sons of noble fathers") were a fairly large group of families, the Bacchiadae of Corinth were a single clan which was jealously exclusive and allowed no marriage with outsiders. The Bacchiadae claimed descent from a Corinthian king named Bacchis. Other ruling aristocracies claimed to be the descendants of the founder of the city, as the Penthilidae of Mytilene from Penthilus son of Orestes. Others again bore titles like Hippeis (Eretria and elsewhere) or Hippobotai (Chalcis), the "horsemen" or "pasturers of horses", an index of their wealth as much as of their noble birth.

Their claim to rule is based on their quality as the *aristoi*, the "best" men, or, to put it another way, on the prestige of their families. The simple equation of good birth with the capacity and the right to rule seemed self-evident to the aristocratic poet Alcaeus of Mytilene in the political poems which he wrote at the beginning of the sixth century. The system was not feudal: the nobles do not hold their land from any central authority, and there is no systematic counter-obligation to clients or adherents. As for the mechanism of government, we hear that the Bacchiadae of Corinth merely took it in turns to exercise the functions of the king for a year, a primitive but possible arrangement. At Athens too the chief magistracies became annual, but here the executive had already been divided: appointment to office is said to have been entirely in the hands of the council known to us as the Areopagus, a descendant of the council of nobles which had advised the king. No doubt there were also councils at Corinth and elsewhere. We hear little of assemblies, which were probably summoned seldom, and not yet anxious to play an active part in politics.

The strength of the aristocracies lay not only in their monopoly of the political machinery, but in their entrenched position in the social and religious structure of the state. Like many other primitive communities, the early Greeks had an elaborate tribal organization, whose relics are still visible in the classical period.

The largest division is the tribe (*phyle*), and the names of tribes are often common to large sections of the Greek race, so that we find in all Dorian states (*see* Chapter V) the three tribes Hylleis Pamphyloi Dymanes, in Athens and in many Ionian states the four tribes Geleontes Hoplethes Aigikoreis Argadeis. These must be original divisions of the larger races, already in existence when they invaded the peninsula and before they settled in their separate cities. Within each state the tribe is subdivided into phratries or "brotherhoods", bearing names which are not like the tribe-names common to a large number of states, and the phratry contains smaller units, clans or groups of families (*genos*). The principle of this structure is the kinship of its members. Not only family, but phratry and even tribe look back to a common ancestor, and if his name is sometimes fictitious the bond of kinship is nevertheless felt as real. A corollary to this, and a tightening of the bond between members of a phratry, is that they share in a common cult.

It is clear that this organization was of the greatest importance to the early Greeks—though we must not carry too far down in their history analogies with the tribal organization of primitive communities among the North American Indians or the Australian aborigines: the interesting thing about the Greeks is not that they began thus organized, but that they largely freed themselves from the system. But it is important to realize that at the beginning it pervaded everything. The army was tribally organized, such political and financial administration as there was depended on kinship groups, and legally they were of great importance in such questions as the pursuit of a murderer or the inheritance of property. Throughout, the system told in favour of the man who could claim noble descent.

The Greek noble was not only a political monopolist but held a privileged position as the controller and expounder of the religious cults of these kinship groups, and as the expounder of the law—or perhaps we should say that these various monopolies still hung together and could not be distinguished. Add to this that early Greek warfare was fought mainly between these nobles, the experts of a somewhat individual and unorganized style of fighting (Chapter III), and it is clear how much the common man was at the nobles' mercy. It is hard to say how well aristocratic government worked. Our knowledge of such matters begins only when it was in decline, with Hesiod's complaint against the grasping injustice of the Boeotian nobles about 700, and the aristocracy had been substantially defeated when the aristocratic poets Alcaeus and Theognis complained of the state of their times in the sixth century. In their best days the nobles were neither mean nor unenterprising. The Bacchiads took the lead in the first great expansion of Corinthian trade and colonization, but this expansion itself unleashed forces which they could not control, and the tyrants represent a revolution against aristocracy.

(c) THE DEVELOPED GREEK CONSTITUTION

The tyrants mark a turning-point between two systems of government, and to understand them we must look also at the system which follows. Briefly, the sovereign body of a developed Greek state is an assembly of all full citizens. In a democracy this means an assembly of all free adult males, whereas under oligarchy the franchise is limited in various ways, originally and most simply by prestige alone, the poor man knowing that political decisions are for his betters to make; but when that can no longer be relied upon, by statutory limitation, most often by making some fixed amount of property the qualification for full citizenship. Government by such an assembly is direct, not as in our large modern states representative, and therefore very different in character from anything we are accustomed to: there is no ministry or "government" to stand or fall, all proposals are debated on the spot by those of the qualified citizens who are willing and able to attend, there are no parties in the modern sense—certainly no enforceable party discipline—and very little in the way of long-term programmes. To an extent which it is physically impossible to achieve in modern conditions, Greek democracy put power directly into the hands of the people, and Greek oligarchy into the hands of a governing class.

But the assembly, though sovereign, could not itself initiate business. This was the function of a smaller council or board of officials, which discussed public business beforehand and then laid its proposals before the assembly for final decision. This preliminary discussion, which the Greeks called *probouleusis*, served to bring some order and continuity into a form of government which might otherwise have lacked either: the assembly, even where it was small, was still too large to deal efficiently with detail, and its vote was very liable to be determined by a rush of temporary emotion (the standard charge against all democratic assemblies). Almost all constitutional governments in Greece followed this pattern of council and assembly, with the difference that in developed democracy the probouleutic body was a large council of ordinary citizens chosen by lot for a year's term, but oligarchies preferred a smaller board with some special qualification, and often chosen for a long term or for life. Further, the practice of oligarchies was to leave public business to the council and magistrates, with the full assembly playing a much smaller part, while in democracies the assembly tended to encroach in every direction[4].

A good deal has been said already of the executive. Lopped of its early powers, subdivided, made annual, subjected to the decisions of an assembly, it was still often potent but looked less and less like the absolute power of early monarchy. Oligarchies usually chose their magistrates by direct election, democracies by the lot, which offered more opportunity to the ordinary man and less to any kind of special influence. Judicial business fell in the first place to the magistrates and councils, who split it between them, but it was characteristic of democracy to allow appeal to a larger court, on the principle of appeal from the expert to the ordinary man. Administration, which could not be reviewed in detail by the full assembly, was subject at Athens to the control of the council—that is, to a representative selection of ordinary citizens.

The concentration of power in the hands of a single tyrant ran counter to the prejudices of those who made and lived under such constitutions as these. Democracy was in a sense more favourable to men of outstanding talent, and needed leaders of ability to give the state direction: but they must be leaders in sympathy with the constitution, and above all they must be removable when the mood and will of the citizens changed— ministers, not masters. Oligarchy, governed mainly by a small council, needed the individual leader less and was more jealous of personal ambition. To both, tyranny was the opposite of a constitution. But the tyrants we are to examine lived before the development of constitutional government of this type, and the problem they present is distinct from the question how a dictator was sometimes able to overthrow the constitution in the classical period.

(d) THE EVIDENCE

Lastly, something must be said of the means at our disposal for examining the early tyrants. The Greeks of the seventh century speak to us in their own persons through their poets and artists, so that we begin already to know what sort of people we are dealing with and what sort of thing occupied their attention. But for a long time yet there were no contemporary historians, and we have no documents of the kind that illumine all but the darkest of our dark ages. The Greeks lost the art of writing early in their dark age, perhaps as early as the twelfth century, and though they learnt to write again in the eighth century, their everyday transactions are lost because the writing materials of that time were not durable in the Greek climate, like the papyri of Egypt and the clay tablets of Mesopotamia[5]. Plutarch has preserved for us one important state document from seventh-century Sparta, but the earliest such document surviving on stone is from the middle of the sixth century, and inscriptions only become common in the middle of the fifth century at Athens.

Herodotus finished his enquiry into the Persian War and its antecedents soon after 430. Though he had some predecessors, he was the first to make a systematic study of such a subject and earned his title of Father of History. His easy manner of explaining matters by digression, as he came to them, has sometimes seemed slipshod to readers accustomed to a different historical technique, but his reputation for incoherence and credulity is undeserved: he lets us down occasionally by his lack of political interest and his tendency to assign trivial and personal motives to political (and even military) action, but his candour and the breadth and warmth of his interests make him an invaluable witness. For the tyrants he gives us oral tradition as it stood in the fifth century. The Peisistratidae were expelled from Athens some twenty-five years, and Polycrates of Samos was killed nearly forty years, before Herodotus was born, so that tradition about them was full and relatively undistorted. The great tyranny of Corinth lay further back—Periander died a full century before Herodotus' birth—and here legend and folk-tale have made serious inroads into the story, as will be seen in Chapter IV.

Oral tradition is liable to these invasions, and after a while begins to confuse even the persons of the story. In the hands of an exacting critic like Thucydides (some twenty years younger than Herodotus) it could be made to yield solid results, but Thucydides' sketch of early history is brief and selective, concentrating on the question of the power developed by Greek states before his own time, and he had no successor of his own calibre. The standard work was written by a very different author, Ephorus of Cyme, whose books on early history were completed by about 340; an industrious, somewhat superficial writer, not unconcerned with truth but at least as much concerned to point conventional moral lessons through a dramatized story. His works are lost, except for fragments, but we can trace his influence in most of the statements made by later writers about this early period.

The remnants of this fourth-century learning are not worthless. It contained some conscious invention, partly to fill gaps in the story (e.g. the account of Cypselus' youth, Chapter III), partly because some issues were seized on for propaganda (especially the early wars between Sparta and Messenia, which became topical when Epaminondas liberated Messenia in 370). But much of Ephorus' material was of the same kind that Herodotus used, and the same canons of criticism apply: we have to judge the probabilities in each case, guessing what is embroidery and what is genuine. The special interests of the fourth century uncovered some new material, for instance in the records of Greek festivals. Ephorus himself collected facts about colonial foundations, and a Corinthian colony would know whether or not it was founded by one of the tyrants.

After the historians come the philosophers, evolving general theories of the nature of tyranny. Plato's classification of constitutions is concerned with their value rather than their history,[6] and though we cannot neglect his influence (Chapter II), we seldom go to him for facts. Aristotle's appetite for concrete instances was greater, and his *Politics* preserve a lot that we should otherwise have lost. His general theory makes the tyrant the champion of the many and the poor against the few and the rich[7]. If a theory is to be framed which shall cover both Cypselus in the seventh century and Dionysius in the fourth, it must be on these lines, making the tyrant the champion of the under-dog, but Aristotle's analysis fits his own time better than it fits the archaic period when the many were still inarticulate. Particular parts of his theory will be discussed as they arise : he is perhaps most convincing when he breaks away from the Platonic caricature of the tyrant as an ogre of wickedness and tries to describe a tyrant whose popularity is intelligible, on the model of Peisistratus.

To regain contact with the seventh century as it really existed, we must go back to the contemporary witnesses. The vase-painters have much to tell us of what they saw around them, and of the myths which were most popular in their time : the rise and decline of the prosperity of particular cities is illustrated by the quantity and quality of their pottery, and the distribution of the places where it has been found. The picture we make of the age of the tyrants must never conflict with this immediate and undistorted evidence, nor with that of the poets.

No narrative poetry described the happenings of that time : the poets who used the Homeric technique were busy with mythology, Hesiod in his *Theogony*, Eumelus in his *Corinthiaca*, and others. Hesiod in grumbling indignation, Solon in a more gracious and reflective but no less painstaking manner, tried to make sense of an imperfect world and of their own conviction of what was right. In the main, the poets of the period express their personal feelings in relation to the facts of their lives. Hesiod sounds this note first, about 700, weaving admonitions to his brother and references to their quarrel into his Farmer's Calendar, the *Works and Days*. Archilochus of Paros and Thasos, in the middle of the seventh century, wrote of his own hates and loves. Sappho, at the beginning of the sixth, moves entirely in a world of private emotion.

Three poets contribute direct evidence for our problem. The Spartan Tyrtaeus, concerned with his city's troubles and not his own, used Homer's vocabulary and the elegiac metre to support the army's morale in the long seventh-century struggle against the Messenian revolt. He is the source of the little we know for certain about that revolt (and about Sparta's conquest of Messenia in the eighth century), and he gives us much-needed help towards solving the Spartan problem discussed in Chapter VI. Alcaeus of Mytilene in Lesbos was obsessed by his own troubles, but his troubles and so his poems were mainly political; an embittered aristocrat, his attitude goes far to explain why his aristocratic world was breaking up around him. Solon of Athens, a moderate and fair-minded man called in 594 to mediate between the parties in a revolutionary situation, addressed his political poems both to his opponents and to his recalcitrant supporters, and his reasons for not wishing to be tyrant help to tell us what a tyrant was. His poems are the most important item among the materials used in this enquiry.

CHAPTER II

THE WORD TYRANT

IT WAS stated in the previous chapter that a tyrant, in Greek terms, is not necessarily a wicked ruler. The statement requires qualification. From early times, as early as the second generation of Greek tyranny, the word was capable of carrying the odium that it carries today, and in the classical period violent emotion could be generated against a man who was suspected of designing to set himself up as tyrant. Yet in other contexts it bears no odium, indeed a monarch might be addressed as "tyrant" in compliment. Again, fourth-century philosophers take it for granted that "king" is the word for a good sort of ruler and "tyrant" for a bad one, yet other (mostly earlier) writers treat the words as synonyms. This is confusing at first sight, but the confusion is not very deep-seated, and a discussion of the Greek use of the word will help to explain how popular rulers like Cypselus or Peisistratus could be classified as tyrants.

The feelings attached to the word king vary widely with the history and political traditions of the people who use it. In circumstances which require a very strong executive, monarchy may be felt as neither good nor bad, but merely necessary. Ithaca, as Homer describes it (p. 10), was helpless without its king, and there are only faint hints in the *Odyssey* that any other kind of government was possible. There have been periods in the history of medieval Europe when one could fairly say that there was no practicable alternative but monarchy or chaos. The need for monarchy among some ancient peoples, in Egypt and the East, went still deeper, or it seemed so to the Greeks: Aristotle treats it as a matter of character rather than circumstance that these barbarians had to have an absolute king[8].

This is perhaps a mere prejudice of the Greek against the foreigner, but it has this much real basis, that the Greeks, or at least the inhabitants of cities with developed constitutions, felt themselves to have outgrown the monarchy which still flourished in other lands. Isocrates expresses this feeling in the pamphlet

which he addressed to king Philip of Macedon, when he alleges
that the original founder of the Macedonian royal house left
Argos and established himself in the barbarian North because he
knew that it was not right or possible to set up a kingdom among
Greeks[9]. When the situation seemed to be too much for the
regularly appointed executive in a Greek city, as at Syracuse
when Dionysius seized power, there were many who submitted
to the supposed necessity with great reluctance, and the tyrant
was always in danger from a liberator. It was a widespread belief
that to kill a tyrant was a virtuous and admirable action.

Loyalty to an established monarchy may survive indefinitely
among peoples who show no tendency to constitutional development, and it has survived such development in England because
the monarchy has adapted itself to change. For many peoples, in
our time and earlier, the survival or restoration of monarchy has
been an actual, acute question, and among them political feeling
can range itself in monarchical and anti-monarchical lines hardly
known in England since the seventeenth century. In Roman
politics, from the expulsion of the Tarquins onwards, the mere
word *rex* aroused prejudice, and the first emperor had to pretend
that he was no more than an unusually influential citizen. The
Greek position is not far from the Roman, but *basileus* had less
sting in it than *rex* because in the end, as we shall see, political
feeling was concentrated on the word tyrant.

(a) TYRANNOS IN VERSE AND PROSE

By a lucky chance we know when *tyrannos* was brought into
the Greek language. The earliest surviving occurrence of it is in
some lines of Archilochus written in the middle of the seventh
century, and Hippias of Elis, writing about 400, tells us that it
was first used in Greek in Archilochus' time. Hippias was a
learned man and had the complete literature available to him, so
he should be right about the fact. The speaker in Archilochus
says, "I do not care about the wealth of Gyges, there is no envy
in me, I am not jealous of the works of the gods, nor do I desire a
great tyranny." Another ancient scholar, probably with this same
passage in mind, asserts that the term *tyrannos* was first applied

to Gyges, a Lydian who in Archilochus' lifetime had killed the king of Lydia and taken the throne for himself. Probably, then, the poet meant his new word to describe the kingdom of Gyges, and it is possible that the word itself was Lydian[10].

Archilochus' speaker certainly thought that a tyranny was something which most men would desire to exercise, but it is not obvious from this fragment alone what precise meaning and colour the word had. Gyges had usurped his throne, which might suggest that *tyrannos* in Greek meant "usurper" from the first, but its use in later poets (*see* below) makes it likely that the meaning was more neutral, in fact that Archilochus used it as a synonym for king.

It comes up next in the poems of Solon, after his settlement of Athens' troubles in 594. He refers more than once to the fact that he might have become tyrant, and from what he tells us about his supporters we can see what tyranny would have meant in Athens then. Their main point was that he had been too lenient with the aristocrats, and had refused to confiscate and redistribute land : they evidently thought of tyranny in terms of Cypselus' revolution sixty years earlier at Corinth, when the main body of the aristocrats had been killed or exiled (Chapter IV), and they wanted the same thing to happen at Athens, but Solon had no personal ambition to be tyrant and recoiled from the bloodshed which tyranny involved. Later in the sixth century Theognis of Megara imitated many of Solon's lines and described in very similar terms the situation of his own city : he was afraid that the troubles of the time would produce a tyranny, and as a survivor of the old aristocracy he found the prospect hateful[11].

Tyranny came to Athens in the end, in spite of Solon, and was not unpopular (Chapter IX), but when the sons of Peisistratus were expelled in 510, the new régime passed laws to prevent its recurrence, and the tyrannicides, Harmodius and Aristogeiton, who had killed Peisistratus' second son Hipparchus in 514, were reverenced as heroes. Since there was this much feeling against even the mild tyranny of the Peisistratids, it is a shock to find that Aeschylus and Sophocles in the fifth century can employ *tyrannos* interchangeably with *basileus*, without apparently feeling that tyrant is at all a derogatory term for the kings of tragedy, or anything but a mere synonym for king[12].

The explanation of this striking fact must lie in the distinction between the vocabulary of verse and the vocabulary of prose. The use of tyrant as a simple equivalent for king must be the original use: it is intelligible that a word might, as it were, go downhill in conversation and in written prose, yet still retain its earlier and better sense in poetry of the elevated style, but it would not be easy to understand how a word with an originally bad meaning could climb up to be innocuous in drama. Probably then Archilochus, when he adopted the word, meant no distinction between *tyrannos* and *basileus*: there were of course several synonyms for king already adopted into the language, but Greek verse with its rigid quantitative metres can always do with another synonym with a different metrical value. Another sign that the word originally can have conveyed no stigma is the fact that in certain religious cults *tyrannos* is the epithet of the god.

In Solon and Theognis *tyrannos* is a derogatory term: their usage and vocabulary are nearer prose, where the word had gone downhill. The adoption of *tyrannos* into prose requires explanation, since prose has not poetry's appetite for synonyms, but it is not hard to see why the spoken language of the late seventh century should have picked up this new poetical word and given it a special sense, for at this precise time there appeared in Greece a new type of monarch for whom a new name was needed, the tyrants who led the revolution against the aristocracy. In the earliest and most spontaneous of these revolutions the tyrant was given power by a popular movement, as in the case of Cypselus of Corinth, but if Cypselus was a beneficent ruler and maybe an honest man, other tyrants were not, and before long they gave tyranny the bad name which has stuck to it ever since. The bad name intrudes even into Attic tragedy, especially with Euripides, and sometimes provides a double meaning.

(b) THE TYRANT'S VIEW OF TYRANNY

In the poems which Pindar wrote for Hieron of Syracuse (tyrant 478–467) he three times calls him king, but once also tyrant, and on this occasion he does not mean to be less polite. This is, up to a point, parallel to the usage of his contemporary

Aeschylus: in their lofty style the words are synonyms, and if Hieron can be called king he can be called tyrant without offence. Nevertheless, in another poem written for an audience of different political complexion, Pindar in set terms expresses his disapproval of tyranny and his preference for the middle road in politics[13]. A century later the eloquent Isocrates wrote an encomium on the Cypriot king Euagoras for his son and successor Nicocles, in which he repeatedly calls Euagoras tyrant and praises tyranny as an institution[14]. But in other writings for other audiences he takes it for granted that tyranny is an evil.

It would be easy to explain this as a mere difference of convention. The Greek world might feel that it had outgrown monarchy, but the writer who addressed a monarch would have to suppress this feeling, and within a court the word tyrant might reasonably retain its original innocence. But the explanation is not quite sufficient: there might be such a court convention to disregard the normal associations of a word, but the Greeks were not given to shutting their eyes in this manner, and the tyrants do not seem much concerned to disguise their position.

We must remember that *tyrannos* was never any man's formal title, and very few tyrants before the Hellenistic age can have supposed that they would gain in constitutional respectability if they were addressed as king. In the very earliest days Cypselus may possibly have regarded himself as a kind of successor to the old kings of Corinth. In his time the hereditary kings had not yet vanished from the Greek scene: apart from Sparta, there was still such a king at Argos in the late seventh century, and when the colony of Cyrene in Africa was founded, as late as *c.* 630, the founder ruled it as king and his descendants after him. At Corinth, as we have seen, the Bacchiadae appointed one of their number every year to hold the position of king, and this provides some continuity in form even though the post had ceased to be hereditary. Cypselus himself was called king of Corinth in a Delphic oracle which must be a contemporary document, and this may be how Cypselus thought of himself, that what he had done was to start a new and more efficient dynasty of kings.

But these are very early days, when the word tyrant itself had only just appeared. Elsewhere the break after the kingly period was complete. Much had happened at Athens, including

the elaborate reforms of Solon, between the last of the kings
and the first tyrant, and though Peisistratus came from an old
family one branch of which had given kings to Athens, and
though he may have lived in the old palace of the kings on the
Acropolis, we shall see him pretending to be no more than a
private citizen ; and he was careful not to disturb the forms of the
Solonian constitution. There is a story that Gelon, who ruled by
conquest at Syracuse, was acclaimed as king by the people after
his defeat of the Carthaginians at Himera in 480, but there are
features in the story that make one doubt it, and it is noticeable
that the Syracusan tyrants take no title in the dedications which
they made at Greek sanctuaries after their great victories, while
the coinage of Syracuse in their time bears the city's name and
not the tyrant's.

Tyranny was not a constitution, and the tyrant held no
official position and bore no formal title. If his courtiers called
him king or tyrant, it was a recognition of his power and enhanced
his prestige, but it made no great difference which word they
used. They were able to use these terms because the tyrant
did not try to conceal the fact of his power, but rather advertised
it, knowing that the ordinary man would at least half admire him
for it.

The average Greek was firmly enough convinced that he
did not want to be the subject of a tyrant, but he was not so firmly
convinced that he would not like to be a tyrant himself, nor could
he withhold his admiration from the man who had succeeded in
making such a position for himself. Several Platonic dialogues
introduce speakers who are sure that a tyrant, however wicked,
must be supremely happy, and it is Socrates' business to persuade
them that the wicked are really miserable. His arguments are
addressed primarily to the young or immature and are based on
the premise that the tyrant in question is obviously and merely
wicked, but the position he attacks was evidently a common one,
and when Isocrates praised tyranny to Nicocles as the greatest
good that could befall a man, he was saying something that would
not seem merely nonsense.

Much of the literature about tyranny is concerned with
the tyrant's exceptional opportunities for sensual pleasure, and
when Solon speaks of his critics who thought him a fool not to

take up the tyranny offered him, it is the material temptations that are in question. Solon preferred to take his pleasures without anxiety, and the greater tyrants, though not austere men, had other things to think of. More serious is the sheer desire for power and the consciousness of capacity to rule, such a belief as I imagine Peisistratus held (and later justified), that he was the man who could put an end to misrule and make Athens happy and prosperous. Such men were conscious of their greatness and were not afraid to have their position described—in the inner councils of Dionysius of Syracuse the word tyrant was freely used—because they believed that what they were doing was worth doing.

In Thucydides' report of his last speech, Pericles compared the Athenian empire to a tyranny, showed his awareness of the danger and unpopularity of Athens' position, but concluded that it was worth while to hold an empire, provided it was a really great empire[15]. However much one may doubt whether even a Greek statesman really made such a comparison in public, or doubt the justice of the comparison, this painfully plain speaking is characteristic of the Greeks' uncompromising approach to such topics. A less brutal and perhaps a better example is the epitaph of Archedice the daughter of Hippias, Peisistratus' son and successor. The first line speaks with pride of her father as "the best man of Hellas in his day", the second couplet claims that she kept her head, though she was the daughter, wife, sister and mother of tyrants[16]. The danger of tyranny to the tyrant is that there is nothing to restrain him from insolence : Archedice could boast that she had avoided this danger, and also boast of the high position which had exposed her to such danger.

(c) HERODOTUS AND THUCYDIDES

We must now turn back to the other side of the picture. It remains true that developed Greek cities were hostile to the idea of monarchy, and this too was an emotion to which political orators could appeal. The hostility is to monarchy as such, and it could make no practical difference whether the monarch was called king or tyrant. A symptom of this is the use of *monarchos* itself, a purely Greek word which is not a title but a noun meaning "sole ruler" : this might be expected to be a neutral term covering all sorts of monarchy good or bad, ancient or modern, and it is used in this neutral way by Aristotle, but to Solon and Theognis a *monarchos* is an evil, the same thing as a tyrant, and this seems to be the normal prose usage outside the philosophers. Another illustration is given by Isocrates in his *Panegyric* published in 380, where he upbraids the Spartans equally for their support of Dionysius the tyrant of Syracuse and of Amyntas the king of Macedon : evidently he can rely on finding in his readers a general dislike of single government as such[17].

These are the sentiments of Herodotus, when he is thinking directly about the subject. The wide sweep of his history brings in many kings, of Cyprus and Macedon, Persia and Egypt, and still more remote places. For none of these does he show much sympathy, unless for Croesus of Lydia, or hostility either : he has not asked himself whether the Cypriots or Macedonians would be happier under another form of government. Nearer home his feelings are more often engaged. He is said to have taken part in the struggle against the tyrants of his native Halicarnassus, and in the case of Athens he expresses his view himself, asserting, beyond what the facts warrant, that the state was weak and distracted under the Peisistratids but became strong and self-reliant the moment the tyranny fell[18].

He makes no firm distinction between the terms he uses. For the old-established kings of the East he usually says king but sometimes tyrant, for the upstart tyrannies of Greek cities mostly tyrant but often king or *monarchos*, and within a single chapter he uses both *tyrannos* and *basileus* for Telys, a late sixth-century ruler of Sybaris whom Aristotle would certainly have classified as tyrant. It is clear that it did not much matter to him which of these words he used, but if he shows a tendency, it is towards the distinction which Thucydides appears to make more precisely.

In his feeling towards tyranny Thucydides stands, as so often, a little apart. With his eye on the question of power and ready to approve any political arrangement that worked effectively, he thought well on the whole of the Peisistratids, but complained of the tyrants in general that they were not powerful or enterprising enough. In the course of his short sketch of early

Greek history he touches on the tyrants, and remarks that before them there were "hereditary kings with fixed privileges" : tyrants, then, are not hereditary and their privilege has no limit[19]. In the rest of his work he has not often occasion to speak of monarchs, but he nowhere breaks through this distinction, and some such differentiation must be the original reason for bringing *tyrannos* into the vocabulary of politics (*cf.* p. 23) : I imagine that if Herodotus had been compelled to distinguish the words, he would have done so on these lines.

Basileus, then, is the appropriate word for the early heredi-tary kings, and for survivals in the direct line of descent like the magistrates called "king" at Athens and elsewhere. Tyrant, which was never any man's title, is the appropriate word for a man who seized power in an irregular way in a modern state. But the distinction was of no very great importance for practical politics, and it was left to the next generation to enlarge and deepen it.

(*d*) PLATO

For Plato the terms are not at all equivalent : king and tyrant are at opposite poles, the philosopher-king the best and happiest of all men, the tyrant the worst and most miserable. No less definitely, though with less abandon, Aristotle dis-tinguishes kingship as the good form of monarchy from tyranny as the bad form, a contrast which Xenophon attributes already to Socrates, his own and Plato's master. This is a real and basic change from the attitude of Herodotus, who died about the year that Plato was born[20].

Theoretical arguments in favour of monarchy had of course been presented earlier. Herodotus himself, in his account of the conspiracy of nobles which set Darius I on the throne of Persia in 522, presents a debate between the conspirators on the future of the Persian constitution, in which he shows that he can appreciate the position of the monarchists, indeed in the historical circum-stances he is bound to let the monarchist Darius win. (The debate is an eccentricity which surprised Herodotus' contemporaries : whatever led him to do it, he has certainly transferred a Greek discussion to an improbable foreign setting[21].) In Plato's time the

common form of monarchical argument is to be found in Isocrates' pamphlets *Philip* and *To Nicocles*, but these are addressed
to king Philip of Macedon and to a Cypriot prince, rulers of
outlying areas where there was a tradition of monarchy, and
neither touches directly the question what might be done in a
developed Greek city nearer home. Even in Aristotle, though he
was Alexander's tutor, the king remains a long way from the
centre of the picture.

Plato, more drastic than these, pushes the contrast of the good
king and the bad tyrant to its limits, turning the tyrant into a
pantomime ogre. He contributed also the famous suggestion that
the Greek cities could be cured of their troubles only by the
appointment of philosopher-kings[22]. The suggestion is in his
political mood : disillusioned as he was about Athenian democracy,
he was no more satisfied with the oligarchs who opposed it, and
was the last man to accept easily the pretensions of the men
who called themselves the "best" people, so that it suited him to
propose a form of government less shop-soiled, less discredited by
the unsuccessful political experiments of the Athenian oligarchs in
his own youth.

Again, the paradoxical form of the pronouncement is in
Plato's own style, for he enjoyed shocking the conventional and
putting his doctrines in a startling form. So here, though the
eventual government of his ideal city is to be aristocratic and it
has no permanent need for the philosophic autocrat, still it
pleases him to bring in the word king, which will certainly arouse
attention. It has often been noted that in the great passage about
the philosopher-kings in the fifth book of the *Republic* Plato
announces his thesis very hesitantly and is very conscious that
he is going to say something strange which will probably be unpopular : the paradox lies not simply in the proposal that philosophers should be entrusted with government, but almost as
much in the proposal that government should be entrusted to
kings[23].

But the more successful a paradox is, the shorter its life as a
paradox and the sooner it is accepted as truth without surprise.
Plato's influence was very great in his own time, the more so that
his disillusionment was not peculiar to himself but widespread
among educated people, and his notion of ideal government by a

virtuous king had its effect on political theorists, an effect which was perhaps all the greater because no one at the time seriously expected the idea to be realized for a Greek city. So the concept of the king was rescued, as far as theory went, from the criticism that monarchs sometimes behave badly. Crimes were committed by tyrants, not kings, and when in real life Macedonian kings conquered the Greek and Asiatic world, there was that much theoretical basis for their acceptance, and an immediate spate of philosophic treatises On Kingship.

(e) CONCLUSION

This discussion has led us some distance from the seventh century, but it serves to show that the contrast, kings are good and tyrants are wicked, was not fully established until the fourth century. Before that, these terms are treated with some indifference, whatever view is being taken of monarchy as an institution, but the beginnings of a distinction are already present, on the line that king is the more usual word for the archaic, hereditary monarchy, while tyrant is the more appropriate word for a modern autocrat. This distinction probably goes back to the early days of tyranny, and arose because it was useful to have a new word for a new phenomenon. But it is not at all regularly observed, and side by side with this poets continued into the fifth century to treat the word tyrant as identical in meaning with king. This was its original meaning, when Archilochus brought it into the language in the lifetime of the earliest tyrants.

CHAPTER III

THE MILITARY FACTOR: PHEIDON OF ARGOS

THE seventh century was a period of many changes in Greece, which will be discussed in this and the following chapters. It might seem more logical to take economic development first, since the other changes all in some measure depend on Greece's growing prosperity: in particular, the cities could not have afforded the military change here described if individual citizens had not grown richer in the last generation or two. This increase in wealth must be kept in mind throughout, but it is easier to deal with economic change when we come to Solonian Athens (Chapter VII), where economic problems are more prominent, whereas the military factor is more relevant to king Pheidon, who conquered half the Peloponnese and is the earliest historical figure with whom we are concerned.

(a) THE HOPLITE ARMY

At the beginning of the seventh century the Greeks changed their style of fighting and began to use the mass formation of heavy-armed infantry called hoplites, the formation which was characteristic of Greek warfare through the classical period and was feared throughout the civilized world. The essential features of the change concern the type of shield, the use of the spear, and the training of a formation instead of individual fighters[24].

In the old style, the spear was a missile weapon, the warrior often carried a reserve spear, and only if he had thrown both without effect did he come to close quarters with the sword. For defence, his body armour was neither heavy nor elaborate, and he relied mainly on a shield with a single handgrip inside at the centre and a strap slung round his neck: if necessary he could

31

leave the shield to hang by its strap and have both hands free, or if he decided to run away he could sling the shield round to protect his back.

In the new hoplite style, defensive armour was much heavier, the main piece being a breastplate of metal, or strips of metal fastened to a background, covering the chest and most of the belly. The shield was held on the left forearm by means of an arm-band inside at the centre, through which the arm was thrust up to the elbow, and a grip for the hand near the rim : there was no strap round the neck. This type of shield was held much more firmly than the older type with the single central grip, but in its normal position it covered only the left side, and it was not easily manœuvred to protect the right. This was not necessary while the line stood fast, for a good half of every man's shield projected to the left of his left elbow and covered the next man's right side. In flight such a shield was no protection at all, merely a burden, and if he ran away the hoplite was apt to throw it down. The spear was still the first weapon of offence, but no longer as a missile : instead, it was held firmly for a thrust, the favourite stroke being made with the spear held high and pointed downwards to attack the neck above the edge of the breastplate. If the spear failed, the hoplite took to his sword like the older type of fighter.

The outstanding difference between the two systems is that hoplites can only fight in formation. Defensively it is clear from the nature of the shield just described that the hoplite's safety depends on the line holding fast. This is what produces the characteristic Greek conception of courage, the picture shown to us by Tyrtaeus and Plato of the good man who keeps his place and does not give ground. Offensively the decisive factor is the weight of the combined charge of several ranks of hoplites with a view to breaking the enemy's line, and this kind of charge needed practice. The old method, on the other hand, led to individual duels of the kind stylized by Homer. When Achilles or Diomede comes forward from the mass of the people, throws his spear at his single adversary, then comes to close quarters with his sword, that is partly due to the exigencies of romantic poetry, Homer's need to keep the limelight on his heroes, but partly also because real fighting of the pre-hoplite period tended to be like that, with the mass of the troops only lightly armed and the expert fighters attacking one another individually.

The painting of battle scenes on Greek pottery begins only in the late eighth century and covers no more than the last phase of this older style of fighting. Many of these pictures are indeterminate, since the front face of the shield is presented and it is impossible to see how it is held, but in some it is clear that the fighter has both hands free, which the hoplite can never have, and in half a dozen examples, pictures or figurines, the shield is unmistakably held out in front by a single handgrip. It is clear how these weapons were meant to be used, and clear that they were being used in the old style at the end of the eighth century.

Fighting between warriors in hoplite armour is depicted on vases from Corinth and Athens before 675, and the series of lead figurines from Sparta shows that hoplite armour was in use there near the beginning of the century. By the middle of the century Protocorinthian artists had mastered the difficult problem of making a picture which represents hoplites in formation : the best-known example is the Chigi vase painted very soon after 650. For purposes of dating, the first representation of even single hoplites is decisive, since the nature of hoplite equipment is such that it must from the first have been used in formation and cannot have been adopted piecemeal. On this basis, we can say with certainty that the hoplite system was adopted in Southern Greece in the first quarter of the seventh century. The same seems to be true of Crete and the islands, but on the mainland of Asia Minor, where conditions were different, the change may have taken place later.

The literary evidence gives a less close date, but Archilochus, who tells us how he threw away his shield in flight, must have had hoplite equipment, and there are clear descriptions of hoplite fighting in the Spartan Tyrtaeus. But Callinus of Ephesus, who strove to rally his countrymen in their fight against the Cimmerians in the middle of the century, speaks only of throwing-spears in the short fragments we have from his elegiacs, and this suggests that the older method persisted on the Asiatic mainland[25].

(b) THE HOPLITE AND THE STATE

The social and political basis for these two styles of fighting must be entirely different. The earlier, more individual method is the method of a military aristocracy, where the mass of the people is of little account and the brunt of the fighting is borne by a class of privileged experts: the hoplite method needs a broader basis, a greater number of trained fighters accustomed to acting as a team and not to showing off their individual prowess. In classical times the hoplites are a sort of middle class, including the more substantial of the small farmers, for the equipment of Greek armies was not provided by the state, and the hoplites were just that income-group which could afford hoplite armour. Thus we might expect, as a political effect of the change to hoplite tactics, that the middle class would start to claim its share of power in the state, breaking into the monopoly held by the aristocrats.

This is very near what Aristotle says about this early period. In two passages of the *Politics* he develops the point that the very early Greek states relied for their main military strength on cavalry, therefore on the wealthy class which could afford to keep horses: therefore, he says, the earliest constitutions after the collapse of the kings were narrow, but when the military strength of the city came to depend on the hoplite army, the basis of the constitution was necessarily widened[26].

The argument is clear and reasonable, but we cannot verify his statement that the early aristocracies relied on cavalry. In some cities the ruling classes bear names that show their interest in horses, notably in the two great cities of Euboea, the Hippeis of Eretria and the Hippobotai of Chalcis (p. 12), but this by itself does not prove that they relied on cavalry. *Hippeis*, the classical word for cavalry, means in Homer the drivers of chariots: the heroes of the *Iliad* did not ride but drove in their chariots to the field and then dismounted to fight on foot, and the early aristocracy of Euboea might have done the same. Among the Greek colonies of Asia Minor cavalry played an important part in the seventh century. These Asiatic Greeks had to fight not only one another but the native kingdoms of the interior, whose forces were mainly horsemen and archers. Mimnermus of Colophon, writing in the latter part of the seventh century, describes by report the prowess of his father in the plain of the Hermus, "breaking the close ranks of the Lydian horsemen" (but apparently himself on foot), and on the Greek side we know that great attention was paid to the cavalry arm in Colophon and Magnesia[27]. In this area the hoplite development came later than it did on the Greek mainland (p. 33), and may have succeeded a phase in which cavalry was of prime importance.

The examples which Aristotle gives of early cavalry fighting are all drawn from these two areas, Euboea and Asia Minor. If they were all his evidence, they will not quite bear his general inference, but he may well have drawn on other early poetry which is lost to us. Greek art of the late eighth century, while it just allows us to distinguish the pre-hoplite method of fighting on foot, does not permit any certain inference about cavalry. We can only say that riding was not a normal accomplishment in the army described by Homer, but was familiar to the generation before Mimnermus. But this uncertainty does not affect the validity of Aristotle's statement that the basis of the constitution had to be broadened when hoplite tactics were introduced. It is certainly true that the pre-hoplite army depended on the narrower circle of an expert aristocracy.

Having spoken of the extension of political power to the hoplites, Aristotle adds the interesting note that this hoplite franchise was called "democracy" by the early Greeks, whereas in his own day it had other names. This is markedly different from the classical sense of democracy, which is conceived on the model of fifth-century Athens and means the constitution in which all free adult males were full voters. The word *demokratia* itself is perhaps no older than the fifth century—that is, than the first institution of democracy at Athens—and it is not very likely that Aristotle had found an earlier use of it in a different sense. More probably he has in mind some shift of the root-word *demos*, a word with a longer history.

Demos, the people, can mean the whole community, including everyone within it whether the community is large or small. It can also mean, not everyone, but the mass of the people in contrast to a privileged class—it can have, that is, a party and not a national sense, an ambiguity that has attacked the word for "people" in many languages. This party sense appears in Solon's poems side by side with the more comprehensive sense, and it was probably in Solon's lifetime, in the early sixth century, that it began to have a party meaning. When Aristotle says that the hoplite franchise was called democracy in these early days, I take him to mean that in some early literature, perhaps in the poems of Solon, *demos* should be understood to refer to the hoplites. At this time the people as a whole had not yet woken up to the part which they might play in politics : opposition to the privileged few came from the wider but still restricted class of the hoplites who were now responsible for the defence of the state.

If *demos* once meant that, the fact has an important bearing on tyranny. It is a commonplace with Greek writers—Herodotus, Plato and Aristotle, to name only the most prominent[28]—that the tyrant begins his career as the champion of the *demos*. This theory of tyranny is held to be true of the earliest as well as the latest tyrants, but it will of course need modification for the early period when conditions were very different from those of Aristotle's day, and it will be a modification in the right direction if we can suppose that these earliest tyrants were champions of the *demos* in the sense that they led the hoplites against the nobles.

(c) HOPLITES AND TYRANNY

In these passages of the *Politics* Aristotle does not connect the hoplites with tyranny, and it is hard to say what particular events he had in mind. But the tyrannies begin a generation or so after the introduction of hoplites, and it is hardly possible that there should be no connection between them.

There is no direct proof that the earliest tyrants, Cypselus of Corinth and Orthagoras of Sicyon, relied on hoplite support. Fourth-century accounts say that both climbed to power by way of military office, but these stories command little confidence. They contain, however, one detail which sounds convincing, that Cypselus never needed a bodyguard, and if this is true he must have been sure of the army. Peisistratus of Athens was beyond doubt a military leader before he became tyrant—Herodotus tells us that he commanded the Athenian army against Megara and captured the Megarian port of Nisaea—but though he was helped at the start by the reputation he had gained in war, it is impossible, as we shall see (Chapter IX), to maintain that he was pushed into power by the hoplites, or by any single discontented class.

The case is clearer when we look at Sparta, where there was no tyranny, and at Solonian Athens, where Solon for a time warded off tyranny. At Sparta more completely than elsewhere the citizens in the classical period were the hoplites: membership of the sovereign assembly depended on one's place, past or present, in the army. These soldier-citizens proudly called themselves the "Equals" (*homoioi*), and while they held down a subject population many times their own number, they attempted to preserve a strict equality within their own body. In Chapter VI it will be maintained that this system was set up by a reform enacted in the seventh century, which was Sparta's answer to the political difficulties of that time. There was no tyranny at Sparta, and one important reason is that they gave the hoplites the vote and insisted on equality between them.

At Athens there was a more genuinely revolutionary situation at the beginning of the sixth century than in Peisistratus' time a generation later. The agrarian distress which led to Solon's appointment as *archon* and mediator in 594, and the reforms which he passed when appointed, will be discussed in more detail in their place (Chapter VII), but one aspect of his constitutional reform must be touched on here. Before his time birth had been the sole criterion of privilege, and the members of the noble families called Eupatridae had controlled the state absolutely. Solon broke this monopoly, and divided the Athenians up, according to their income in kind, into four classes with graduated privileges. The largest and lowest class in this new timocratic state was given only what Aristotle calls the bare minimum of power, the right to vote in the assembly and at elections, and to sit in the court of appeal. High office was restricted to the two richest classes. In between comes the third class called *zeugitai*, who were roughly the hoplites, indeed that seems to be the meaning of the name: they were admitted to minor political office. Solon did not simply transfer power from one class to another, but distributed it between his four classes.

His later poems, written after he had laid down office, are mostly addressed to what he calls the *demos*, which was evidently disappointed and resentful at the moderation of his reform, having hoped for the complete expropriation of the nobles' land and its distribution to themselves. It cannot be claimed that in these poems *demos* means literally the hoplites and no one else, but the hoplites were the politically active element, the group who would have gained most land if there had been a revolution. Solon, as he boasts, contrived to keep the *demos* in order. In his constitutional settlement the principal gainers were the rich men outside the circle of the great Eupatrid families. The hoplites got only as much as Solon thought good for them, and it was not nearly as much as they wanted. But his complex and moderate settlement secured Athens for the time being from tyranny.

In many other cities there were revolutions, and the transfer of power was carried through more crudely. It would be unprofitable to discuss the less well-known states in detail, but in general, looking not only at the tyrannies but at the régimes which succeeded them, the total effect of the episode of tyranny was to take power from the narrow aristocracies and to leave it in the hands of a much wider class. The detailed evidence sometimes confirms and nowhere contradicts the thesis that these were mainly hoplite revolutions, and the *a priori* likelihood is very great that the institution of the hoplite army would entail such a shift of political power.

It would be wrong to stress exclusively the military side of this process by which the Greeks grew up politically, for the military system was only one of the things that needed altering. But it was a reform urgent everywhere at the same time, since in military development no state can afford to lag behind, and if one city adopted the new arms and tactics the rest must do so in self-defence. From now on the defence of the state rested on the hoplites, and with the knowledge of this it is not surprising that they should gradually acquire confidence and begin to demand a share of political power.

(d) KING PHEIDON OF ARGOS

If we ask where this development began, the answer is very probably Argos, not because the archaeological evidence points particularly in that direction, but because it was in the early seventh century that Argos enjoyed a brief ·revival of military power and for once defeated Sparta in war, under that king Pheidon who according to Aristotle exceeded the traditional bounds of royal power and made himself tyrant. We have to account both for this sudden display of Argive strength and for the special position ascribed to Pheidon, and both can be explained if we suppose that Argos was first in the field with the new tactics and so gained a temporary advantage.

We have an odd document of this phase of Argivè history in a poem quoted in the Palatine Anthology[29] and elsewhere, which is classified as an oracle, but seems rather to fall into three distinct sections of different date and character, which I give separately:

> "The best of all land is the Pelasgian plain: best are the horses of Thrace, the women of Sparta, and the men who drink the water of fair Arethusa [the men of Chalcis in Euboea].
> But better still than these are the dwellers between Tiryns and Arcadia of the many sheep, the linen-corsleted Argives, the goads of war.
> But you, men of Megara, are neither third nor fourth nor twelfth, nor of any place or account at all."

This poem is certainly early, for from the sixth century onwards the Spartan army was pre-eminent, but here Spartan women are praised and the army of another state. It refers to the historical period and not to the world of mythology, since it places Argos on its classical site between Tiryns and the Arcadian border, which became the centre of the Argolid only in the historical period. It is the illogicality of the second section that impels one to break the poem up, for there is no sense in naming the best, and then adding something that is better still. The first section once stood alone, a proverbial list of excellent things. The second and more discursive section was added in honour of Argos when Argos had eclipsed Chalcis in military power. The third section is a joke in the form of a Delphic response, against Megara or any other city whose name would fit: another version names Aigion.

The eclipse of Chalcis by Argos is a conjunction only possible at the beginning of the seventh century. Chalcis and Eretria, the two great cities of Euboea, had fought in the late eighth century a war, known generally as the Lelantine war from the plain of Lelanton which lies between them. Thucydides tells us that this early war, more than any other, divided the rest of Greece into two alliances, and it may fairly be called the first military event of any scale and importance in the Greek historical period. Eretria suffered no lasting damage, and her allies in the East gained from the war, but Chalcis won at least one important victory in Euboea, and with her ally Corinth she secured the upper hand in the West[30]. This is the time when Chalcis founded her western colonies, Leontini and Catana, which share the fertile corn-plain of north-east Sicily, Rhegium and Zancle (Messana), which control the sea passage between Italy and Sicily, all of them shortly before or after 730. The men of Chalcis might well rank high at the end of the century.

The rise of Argos under king Pheidon comes soon after 675. Two facts about him stood out for Herodotus, who mentions them only in passing to identify a certain Leocedes as this Pheidon's son: his sacrilegious seizure of Olympia and his establishment of a system of measures for the Peloponnese. Later writers add that he robbed the Spartans of their hegemony of the Peloponnese, that he recovered what they call the "heritage of Temenus", that he invented weights as well as measures and was the first to coin silver[31]. This last can hardly be true, but the rest has some meaning, and the sequence seems to be as follows.

In 669 an Argive army defeated the Spartans near Hysiae in the hollow of the mountains on the road which leads up from the Argive coast to Tegea in Arcadia. Hysiae is on the Argive side of the border, so the Spartans were the invaders, though it would be premature to credit them with a hegemony of the Peloponnese so early. The defeat must have been heavy, for in

the next year Pheidon was able to march right across the Peloponnese, seize Olympia from the Eleans and celebrate the festival
under his own presidency. At the height of his power he controlled a large part of the Peloponnese. Temenus, the founder
of Dorian Argos, was supposed in the legend (Chapter V) to
have divided most of the Peloponnese with his two brothers:
he took Argos and the north-eastern cities, and it is this domain
which Pheidon is said to have reunited. We find traces of him
probably at Epidaurus and Aegina, less certainly at Phlius and
Sicyon. At Corinth, which stood outside the Temenus legend,
we have stories of Pheidon plotting against the city, and the
statement that he met his death intervening on behalf of his
friends in an internal fight at Corinth.

A Pheidonian system of measures certainly existed, and
was still known and used in the fourth century, but there is no
trace of a Pheidonian weight standard, and he lived too soon to
have struck coins. Ancient tradition knows other claimants for
the invention of coinage, but we may believe Herodotus that he
imposed on his domains the measures which bore his name.

Such literary description as we have is not enough to determine
whether the fighting between Chalcis and Eretria in the Lelantine
plain was of the hoplite or the pre-hoplite type[32], and we have no
description at all of Pheidon's style of fighting. But the dates of
the Lelantine war and of the reign of Pheidon, if they are correctly
given above, suggest that the Chalcidians were the last great
exponents of the older style and the Argives the first successful
exponents of the new, and this suggestion would account for the
language of the "oracle". If the Argives were the first to adopt
the new tactics, that gave her army the temporary advantage which
Pheidon exploited in this last flowering of Argive power. In the
next century Sparta took the lead, and Argos never recovered it.

The hoplites may also account for the fact that Pheidon is
classified as a tyrant. Aristotle gives no details, merely mentions
him as an example of a king who exceeded his hereditary powers
and made himself tyrant. (The fact that Herodotus refers to
him as tyrant has no significance: *see* p. 27. There need be no
doubt that he was in fact the hereditary king.) Ephorus (p. 17),
who is probably Aristotle's authority, said that the kings of
Argos were reduced to mere figureheads, as early as the grandson

of the founder Temenus[33], and there is no difficulty in believing that effective power was in the hands of the aristocracy in the eighth century. But Pheidon was clearly no mere figurehead, and we are bound to ask how he was able to make himself the effective ruler.

If it was he who organized the new hoplite army, the question is easily answered. The adoption of the new system was bound to diminish the relative importance of the nobles, and the successful leader of such an army might well gain power at home as well as success abroad. Thus, even if he never heard the word *tyrannos*, Pheidon may really be a precursor of the tyrants and exemplify the thesis that their support came from the hoplites.

CHAPTER IV

THE OVERTHROW OF AN ARISTOCRACY
AT CORINTH

THE aspect of Cypselus' tyranny[34] which emerges most distinctly
from the ancient accounts is that the Bacchiadae whom he
overthrew were a harsh, oppressive and unpopular aristocracy,
whereas his own rule—though Herodotus says otherwise—was
well liked in the city. The revolution at Corinth was both the
first and, as it were, the purest of its kind, the aristocrats ripe for
their downfall, the tyrant a straightforward liberator, so much
identified with his supporters that he never needed a bodyguard.
His son Periander made more noise in the world and built up his
own and Corinth's power to great heights, higher indeed than
the basis would stand : within a few years of his death the tyranny
collapsed, and Periander himself was execrated by posterity as
the type of the wicked tyrant. For all that, posterity never re-
habilitated the Bacchiadae, and the memory of Cypselus' mildness
remained.

(a) THE BACCHIAD ARISTOCRACY

Corinth was marked out to be a rich city, and "rich" is its
stock epithet in poetry. The two sheltered gulfs east and west
make it a natural meeting-point for maritime trade, and Thucydides points out that even before the Greeks took to the sea
Corinth's position on the isthmus, across the land route between
mainland Greece and the Peloponnese, ensured its prosperity as a
market. This position was not however exploited on any large
scale until the second half of the eighth century—that is, not until
a time when the Bacchiadae were in control. There are earlier
symptoms of an interest in the West, but it is now that the big
expansion of the western trade begins. After the middle of the
century Corinthian pottery appears in the East at Posideion, the

Greek city at the mouth of the Orontes on the natural route to
Mesopotamia. By this route Corinthian artists were brought into
direct contact with the art of the East, which gave the impulse to
the Protocorinthian style of pottery, a finished style with a
strength and certainty, a grace and lightness, which no contemporary Greek fabric can match[35].

The Bacchiadae were leaders of Corinth's eighth-century
expansion. The two great western colonies were founded by
Bacchiad nobles, Syracuse by Archias and Corcyra by Chersi-
crates, both about 734. Another Bacchiad was Eumelus the poet,
who gave the Corinthian legends their established form, an
earlier contemporary working in the same field as Hesiod (p. 18),
but his works could not compete with Hesiod's and are now lost:
the fragments show, among much else, Corinthian interest in the
Black Sea area colonized by Miletus. Towards the end of the
century Corinth and Samos took part in the Lelantine war
(p. 40) on the side of Chalcis: a Corinthian shipwright built for
the Samians four warships in a new style invented at Corinth,
and the Corinthians at Corcyra expelled some Eretrian colonists
who had settled there first. It seems to be in the colonial sphere
that Corinth gained most from the war, and from this time
begins her long predominance in the western trade. These were
the great days of the Bacchiadae. "Wealthy and numerous and
nobly born," as the geographer Strabo says[36], drawing perhaps on
Ephorus, "they took their toll of the market without stint," and at
the end of the eighth century it was a market worth exploiting.

Fifty years later the picture is no longer the same. About 700
or a little later come the exploits of the Megarian leader Orsippus,
whose tombstone boasts that he retrieved for his country much
border land which enemies had cut off[37]. Corinth's position must
have been weakened in other directions by the growth of Argive
power under Pheidon in the second quarter of the century. In
664 comes a sea battle between Corinth and Corcyra which
Thucydides tells us was the oldest sea battle he knew of: austerely
confining his interest to the fact that naval activity was increasing,
he does not say what the battle was about or even who won it,
but that it should happen at all shows that the Bacchiadae had
lost control of Corcyra[38].

Thus, even before Cypselus appeared, the aristocrats who

had led the city towards greatness and prosperity could no longer justify their rule by success. It is not surprising that the Corinthians, whose achievements under the tyranny show their continuing energy, began to resent the Bacchiadae as parasites and their rule as a restraint. It is no doubt mainly from this last period of their rule that they gained their reputation as harsh oppressors.

(b) CYPSELUS' REVOLUTION

We have two main accounts of the rise of Cypselus: one from Herodotus who regards him as a monster, while the other, which is found in several sources and can be traced back to Ephorus, is favourable to Cypselus but very hostile to his son.

Herodotus puts his version into the mouth of a Corinthian delegate whose business is to persuade the Spartans of the detestable nature of tyranny, which he does by telling the story of Cypselus and Periander, setting them in the worst possible light. He devotes few words to the opening situation, merely stating the fact of Bacchiad rule and adding, because he needs this detail for his story, that they married only inside their clan. But Labda, a Bacchiad daughter, was lame and none of the clan would have her, so she was married to Aëtion, whose descent was from Caeneus and the Lapithae. Cypselus was their son, and on account of certain oracles the Bacchiadae resolved to destroy him, but the baby was concealed from them in the chest (*kypsele*) from which he then took his name. All this Herodotus tells at length, in pleasantly fairy-tale style, then becomes once more very brief. Cypselus grew up, obtained an oracle from Delphi (*see* below), attempted and won his tyranny. Nothing is said about the means by which he rose to power, but once there "he exiled many, deprived many of their goods, most of all of their life". Then after thirty years' rule he died, handing on his tyranny to his son Periander, who began more mildly but finished by becoming bloodier than his father.

Ephorus' version pays more attention to the mechanism of his rise. After his escape from the Bacchiadae the baby was sent abroad; returning as a man he gained great popularity by his virtues and his unlikeness to the wicked Bacchiadae, so he was elected polemarch. This should be a military office, but we hear only of civilian functions, how he increased his popularity by his kind treatment of debtors, formed a party, killed the last reigning Bacchiad, and was made king in his stead. He recalled those whom the Bacchiadae had exiled, sent his enemies out to the colonies he founded, exiled the Bacchiadae, and confiscated their property. In conclusion, "Cypselus ruled Corinth mildly, maintaining no bodyguard and enjoying the good will of the Corinthians." Periander however by his brutality and violence turned the kingship into a tyranny, and had a bodyguard.

The mechanics of the story are not really improved in this version. It would suit the thesis of the last chapter if we could believe that Cypselus rose to power by way of military office, but the details are unconvincing: it is disappointing to hear nothing of the military side of the polemarchy, and the civil arrangements described sound very unlike the seventh century. Tradition had left a gap here, as Herodotus does, and probably the fourth-century historians felt the gap and filled it with fiction which conformed to the preconceptions of their own time. There is more to be said for the sympathy shown in this version to Cypselus personally. In so far as this runs counter to the conventional conception of the wicked tyrant, it is less likely to be fiction and more likely to repose on genuine tradition, and the detail that Cypselus needed no bodyguard sounds authentic. More important, there are elements in Herodotus' version which run counter to his interpretation of the characters of the story.

In the first place there is the fairy-tale, which occupies the main part of Herodotus' chapter on Cypselus, presumably because he liked it as a tale. In this as in many similar tales, the baby is evidently the hero and the nobles who wish to kill it are the villains. Such a story cannot have been meant for a version in which Cypselus was the villain. More important still, because they are public documents, are the oracles which Herodotus quotes. First are the two at the beginning which made the Bacchiadae resolve on Cypselus' death. One was addressed to his father:

"Aëtion, no one honours you though you deserve much honour. Labda is with child, and she shall bear a great rock, which will fall upon the rulers and set Corinth to rights."

This was friendly to Aëtion and might well alarm the nobles. The second, said to have been given to the Bacchiadae earlier, is in a different style:

"An eagle [aëtos, i.e. Aëtion] has conceived in the rocks [petrai, said to be the name of Aëtion's village], and shall bear a strong devouring lion: he shall loose the knees of many. Take heed now of this, Corinthians who dwell round fair Peirene and the cliffs of Corinth's citadel."

This is more conventional oracular stuff, less tied to the actual situation: it is hostile to Cypselus. Third is the one with which Cypselus was greeted when he entered the shrine at Delphi:

"Happy is the man who now enters my house, Cypselus son of Aëtion, king of famous Corinth—himself and his children, but his children's children no longer."

The first two lines read like deliberate encouragement to Cypselus to seize the throne. The third was fulfilled when his grandson was killed in a counter-revolution after only three years' reign, and it would not be unreasonable scepticism to suppose that it was added after that event: it is loosely enough attached in the original.

The fairy-tale and the friendly oracles agree very ill with the general tendency of Herodotus' account, and we can best explain their presence in his text by supposing that they were already traditional elements in the story before his time, and that he took them over without quite noticing how they told against his speaker's view of Cypselus. In that case the tradition found in later writers of the mild and popular Cypselus is the earlier version, and Herodotus' treatment of him is a perversion of the usual story. (Periander is another matter.)

In the case of the oracles we can go further. The Delphians were certainly on good terms with Cypselus during his tyranny, when he made rich dedications at the sanctuary and built what was perhaps the first of those "treasuries" often built by the richer cities to hold their offerings[39]. It is not likely that they quarrelled with the great Periander in the days of his power : if they had, we should not have been allowed to forget it. But as a result of transactions to be described in the next chapter, Delphi had turned against the Cypselids before their fall in 582, and when the Corinthians of the new régime asked permission to erase Cypselus' name from his treasury and substitute the city's, Delphi granted the request as just, though a similar request was rejected by the Eleans as regards Olympia[40].

The second of the oracles quoted above is hostile to Cypselus and seems to be a product, though not a specially highly coloured one, of Delphi's later attitude, when the oracle was concerned to maintain that it had always both foreseen and disapproved. The others must be earlier, and must rank as the earliest literary documents that we have for Cypselus. From an early stage, perhaps even before the revolution, Delphi took sides with Cypselus against the Bacchiadae, and though Delphic approval is not infallible proof that Cypselus was a good man, it is a powerful contribution to the belief that he was popular in Corinth in his time.

Something has been said already of the Bacchiad system of government. Of the authors dependent on Ephorus, Diodorus says that the Bacchiadae as a whole were the governing class, and that they appointed one of their number every year to fill the position of king. Both he and Pausanias[41] refer to this annual officer as *prytanis*, the title of a magistrate (often the chief magistrate) in many classical cities and one of the numerous equivalents for "king" in verse. Nicholas of Damascus actually refers to the last Bacchiad as reigning. There will of course have been subsidiary officers and a council, but these brief descriptions suggest that the political machinery of the monarchy was not much changed by the Bacchiadae, and that their annual magistrate was not so different from a king that the continuity of the system was broken. In that case it is possible, as has been suggested (p. 24), that Cypselus regarded himself as a new heir to the old monarchy.

The revolution was nevertheless a radical change. The governing class had been broken, and Cypselus' council and minor magistrates will have been drawn from a new class not previously concerned with government. The rapid growth of Corinthian power and prosperity shows that there were men available to run this new government, and the explanation of this fact must be sought in the activity of preceding generations. The expansion of commerce had brought wealth to others besides the Bacchiadae, and these outsiders were ready to let their weight be felt in politics. The hoplites had had time to gain self-confidence and can hardly have been left out of the new system : if Cypselus had no bodyguard, it shows that he could rely on the army.

Other factors may contribute to his rise, for instance national resistance to Pheidon of Argos : Pheidon is said to have been killed in a civil disturbance in Corinth[42], and since both his death and Cypselus' accession must come about the middle of the century, the disturbance could have been an incident of Cypselus' revolution. It will be discussed in the next chapter whether racial feeling was a factor : the Bacchiadae were Dorians, Cypselus' father non-Dorian, but at Corinth this can hardly have been the main consideration. The main impression remains, that the Bacchiadae were hated and the liberation of Corinth was welcomed.

(c) THE TYRANTS IN POWER

The internal revolution which began Cypselus' reign was also its main event, for his policy was peaceful abroad as well as at home, and in his day the external danger receded. The rise of the independent national tyrannies of the Isthmus states, Sicyon and Epidaurus as well as Corinth, set free territories which Pheidon had dominated, and for the rest of the century it is likely that Argos had her hands full fighting Sparta. Megara gave no further trouble. Theagenes' tyranny there, set up not long after Cypselus', is known to us only as a revolt against the rich in which their flocks were slaughtered, and from Theagenes' attempt to set up his son-in-law Cylon as tyrant of Athens[43]. The Megarian tyranny was in the same style as the Corinthian, and the two may have been on friendly terms.

Cypselus' positive activities lie to the north-west, where he and Periander planted several Corinthian colonies, Leucas Anactorium and Ambracia, and further north Apollonia and Epidamnus (Dyrrhachium or Durazzo), which spread Corinth's influence all up this north-western coastline. The effect was not only to safeguard the route to Italy and the West, but, still more important, to open up trade with the interior. We find Corinth exporting prefabricated terracotta revetments for a temple at Calydon in Aetolia, and further north exploiting the route across the top of the peninsula which in Roman times became the Via Egnatia : a striking find of early Greek bronzes at Trebenishte, halfway along this route, means either that Corinthian merchants travelled there, or more probably that the rich princes of the neighbourhood made their purchases in Epidamnus or Apollonia, the Adriatic terminals of the route. (The princes of Lyncestis above Macedonia later claimed descent from the Bacchiadae, which suggests that Corinthian influence had penetrated this area before the tyranny.) It is also possible that Corinth obtained silver from the North : the latest study of the mines of Damastion, though it locates them a long way east from the Adriatic coast, still allows this possibility. These are only samples from a large mass of material illustrating the extent and importance of Corinth's connection in this area, the most durable and valuable legacy left by the tyrants[44].

Periander's more warlike influence was felt more widely. His closest political friendship was with Thrasybulus the tyrant of Miletus—the alignment of the greater cities had changed since the Lelantine war, when Corinth and Miletus were on opposite sides—and this friendship will have assisted Corinthian traders in Egypt and on the Black Sea coasts, and Milesian traders in the West. He was called in to arbitrate a dispute between Mytilene and Athens over Sigeum in the Troad, and in effect adjudged it to Athens[45] : the later friendship between Corinth and Athens has its roots in Periander's reign, and is based on the fact that they were beginning to have a common enemy in Aegina. Nearer home he annexed Epidaurus, dispossessing the tyrant, his own father-in-law Procles. He planted a colony in the north Aegean at Potidaea in an area otherwise filled by Euboean colonies : this may be connected with the overland route from the Adriatic, for though Potidaea is not at the point where this road reaches the Aegean, it is in a strong position not far away. It is possible that he intervened in Euboea itself. Four contemporary lines by an unknown poet complain of the ravaging of the Lelantine plain (p. 40) and of revolution in the city, coupling this with a curse on the Cypselidae, and the simplest explanation is that Periander had supported revolution in one of the cities of Euboea[46].

It is a symptom of Periander's position in the Greek world that he maintained relations with powerful foreign kings outside it. He sent presents to Alyattes king of Lydia, and it is probably because of this friendship that most of the dedications made at Delphi by the Lydian kings stood in the treasury originally built by Cypselus. The last tyrant of Corinth, Periander's nephew, was called Psammetichos, the Greek form of the name Psamtek borne by three kings of the contemporary XXVI dynasty in Egypt. The Greek colony of Naucratis in Egypt was founded early in Periander's reign, an East Greek city in which Aegina alone of the cities of old Greece took part, but Corinthian pottery is found there in its early days[47].

Of his home government we cannot form so clear a picture. Periander became the type of tyranny, and Aristotle, for instance, says that he was the author of most of the conventional devices by which tyrants repress their subjects—suppression of outstanding personalities, forbidding the citizens to live in the city, sumptuary legislation, prevention of assemblies, anything that will keep the city weak and divided. But the force of the convention distorts the picture, as is clearly seen in Aristotle's treatment of the public works which were a feature of every tyranny, when he takes the Cypselid works as the standard instance, and concludes that "all these things have the same force, to keep the subjects poor and occupied"[48]. Occupied perhaps, but hardly poor in the case of Periander's Corinth: the tyrant's building programmes, like Pericles' later, were an end in themselves and tended to the greater glory of the city, and if they had any further purpose in home politics they might as reasonably be called a full employment policy. But the conventional view finds sinister motives everywhere and repeats the same charges monotonously against each tyrant, so that it is hard to be sure what we may believe of Periander, or how to interpret what we do believe.

His revenge on Corcyra after a revolt in which his son was killed was brutal enough: 300 Corcyrean boys were sent as a present to Alyattes to be made eunuchs, but were rescued on the way by the Samians—a notorious public case, where the facts cannot be mere invention. Another public action is his annexation of Epidaurus and expulsion of his father-in-law Procles—but here we reach the fringes of his domestic saga, how he killed his wife and quarrelled with his sons, where fact and fiction are hard to distinguish and folk-tale certainly has some part. It is likely enough that Periander was something of a brute. Certainly he was a powerful and energetic ruler, unlike his father a man of war, who kept a fleet on both seas, east and west, and made continual expeditions apart from the particular cases already enumerated. So he built up for himself and his city a great position in the world. He was such a man as his subjects both boast of and complain about, fighting for him today, but ready perhaps to rebel tomorrow against him or his successor.

His reputation was not all dark, in his own day or later. The meagre epitome which is all that remains of Aristotle's *Constitution of Corinth* begins with a catalogue of his tyrannical methods, but ends by saying that "he was moderate in other ways, especially in his taxation, and contented himself with market and harbour dues"[49]. A persistent tradition numbers him among the "Seven Wise Men" of Greece, though some found this irreconcilable with his character as tyrant and excluded him; unjustly, for the Seven were not philosophers in any Platonic sense, but very practical sages, and Periander's undoubted practical ability entitles him to his place, while the contemporary view of tyranny would not disqualify him[50]. Nevertheless his great reign over-strained Corinth, preparing his successor's downfall, and in the following centuries Corinth steadily declines in power.

While he lived Corinth prospered, and the tyrant kept magnificent court. Arion the poet from Lesbos was his guest, and developed the poetic form called the dithyramb: Pindar makes both the dithyramb and the Doric order of architecture Corinthian inventions[51]. The Protocorinthian style in art did not last very long beyond the accession of Cypselus, but its successor, the style we call Corinthian, had its different virtues and was made and exported in increasing quantities, giving way to the products of Athens only in the latter part of the sixth century, when Periander was some time dead. We can only guess at the progress of large-scale painting and the other arts, but we know enough to be sure that Periander justified his reputation for magnificence.

CHAPTER V

THE RACIAL FACTOR:
CLEISTHENES AND OTHERS

SOME Greek peoples claimed that they had always lived in the same land and recognized no distinction of race among themselves, while in other states there was an unforgotten division between the original inhabitants and their later conquerors. The Arcadians, pent in historical times in the mountains of the central Peloponnese, seem in fact to have been a more or less homogeneous people. Attica was more open to the world and boasted of her past hospitality to every kind of refugee, but still the Athenians felt themselves to be a single race and were proud of being in the Greek phrase *autochthonous*, sprung from the soil of their land. On the other hand the Dorians, the latest of the Greek races to enter the Greek peninsula, preserved a memory of their invasion of the Peloponnese, where they partly subjected, partly drove out their predecessors.

(a) THE DORIANS IN THE PELOPONNESE

The Dorians felt the need to legitimate their conquests, so they said that their ancestors had come to take up an inheritance left them by Heracles, who had held these lands in earlier days. So there grew up, in its various forms, the legend of the Heraclidae and their return to the Peloponnese, which was then divided between three brothers, Heracles' descendants: Argos and the north-east to Temenus the eldest, Messenia to Cresphontes, Sparta to Aristodemus or his twin sons. The legend covers those parts of the Peloponnese where the Doric dialect was spoken in classical times: Argos, Corinth, Sicyon, Epidaurus and the minor cities of the north-east, Sparta and Laconia, Messenia. (Corinth, which seems to have broken away from an original dependence on Argos, developed a separate legend and a

54

separate Heraclid founder, Aletes.) Doric was also spoken in Crete, in Rhodes and the south-east corner of Asia Minor, and in the islands of the southern Cyclades which form a bridge between the Peloponnese and Rhodes: most of these asserted a connection with Heracles. Only in the case of Messenia is there any doubt that this distribution of legend and dialect corresponds to a real distinction of race[52]. In the north-west Peloponnese the Eleans spoke a dialect closely akin to Doric, and there is no doubt that the Eleans are late conquerors also. The legend could not call them Dorians, but it fitted them in by saying that their founder Oxylus had guided the Heraclidae back to the Peloponnese and had been rewarded with the gift of Elis.

By the end of the migrations and the beginning of the history of Greece as we know it those pre-Dorian peoples of the Peloponnese who retained their independence at all had been pushed back to the west coast or into the Arcadian mountains. Near the end of the eighth century the process was taken a stage further when the Spartans completed the conquest of Messenia. In the conquered areas the pre-Dorians were mostly reduced to serfs; most notoriously the helots who served the Spartans, but we hear also of *gymnetes* at Argos, "club-bearers" at Sicyon, "dusty-feet" at Epidaurus and others who are compared to the helots and described as a class between slave and free[53]. But not quite all the pre-Dorians were treated in this way. In the classical period most Dorian states possess, besides the three old Dorian tribes Hylleis Pamphyloi Dymanes (p. 13), a fourth tribe whose name varies, Hyrnathioi at Argos, Aigialeis at Sicyon, various other names at Epidaurus and in the Cretan cities. These extra tribes seem to contain non-Dorians who were admitted as citizens. It is not easy to say when they were formed and when these non-Dorians acquired political rights, but already in the seventh century Cypselus' father Aëtion was a non-Dorian with some standing. The descendant of Caeneus, who married even a lame Bacchiad, was not a serf, and his position shows that some of the upper classes of the conquered had gained a place in the social scheme, if not a share in the government.

Cypselos was non-Dorian on his father's side, and the oracle cited on page 47 began by saying that Aëtion received less honour than he deserved: this might be an indication that

Cypselus led a revolt of the conquered against their Dorian conquerors. The Sicyonian tyrants were also of non-Dorian origin, and Cleisthenes went out of his way to stress the fact. The "Pisatan" tyranny seems to be based on a reaction against the Eleans, and Messenian resistance to Sparta might also be seen as part of a widespread anti-Dorian movement in the second half of the seventh century. Such a general movement would be a natural reaction against the aggression of Pheidon, the king of Dorian Argos. But the cases must be examined individually to see what they are worth.

(b) CORINTH

We can only guess at the decisive factor in Corinth, that is the proportion between Dorians and non-Dorians at the time of the revolution, and the proportion between Bacchiadae and other Dorians. Unless the Dorians of Corinth were a very small minority, a single clan cannot form the whole body of them, and more probably the Bacchiadae were only a small fraction. (It is significant that they take their name from a king later than the Dorian founder Aletes.) We cannot tell the proportion of non-Dorians at all, and even tribe-names are no help here, since the original tribe-division of Corinth was obliterated by a new system of eight tribes set up when the tyranny fell[54].

But it is clear enough from the story that the revolution of Cypselus was aimed at the Bacchiad clan rather than at the Dorians as such. The most likely answer is that he had Dorian as well as non-Dorian supporters, and that the two racial groups were to some extent fused in hostility to the Bacchiads. The revolution is perhaps the moment when some non-Dorians gained equality of status with the Dorian citizens, thus remedying the grievance which the oracle ascribes to Aëtion, and the re-division into eight tribes after the tyranny was no doubt intended to make an end of racial differences. But the evidence does not here suggest that a racial grievance was the mainspring of the whole revolution.

(c) THE ORTHAGORIDS OF SICYON

The evidence of racial feeling at Sicyon relates to Cleisthenes in the early sixth century and not to Orthagoras who founded the dynasty in the middle of the seventh. The standard story about Orthagoras' accession is that the Delphic oracle told a Sicyonian embassy that the city must be scourged for a hundred years: whoever on returning first heard that a son had been born to him, that son was to be the tyrant who would do the scourging. With the embassy was a cook named Andreas, and inevitably the noble Sicyonians overlooked him and his son Orthagoras, who duly became the tyrant[55]. A folk-tale of a familiar type has taken charge here, and the hundred years are not likely to be a genuine prediction before the event: the story is a specimen of the later re-editing of Delphi's views when the Sicyonian tyranny had been overthrown by Sparta. Even the suggestion that Orthagoras, unlike Cypselus or Peisistratus, was a man of the people is not to be relied on in view of the ingrained Greek habit of attributing low birth to a political opponent.

Nor do we gain much from a papyrus fragment of Ephorus, or a related historian[56], which tells how Orthagoras in spite of his birth distinguished himself in youth among the frontier guards against the neighbouring Achaean city of Pellene, rose to command these guards, gained the people's favour and became polemarch. This is better than the parallel account of Cypselus (p. 46) in that the polemarch has at least a military career, but it still sounds like a fourth-century attempt to fill a gap.

More to the purpose is the fact that the Orthagorids receive from Aristotle the same friendly judgment that he gives to Cypselus: they were mild, almost constitutional rulers and this is why tyranny lasted so long at Sicyon. Here the parallel case of Cypselus makes the judgment more, not less, convincing. It is again relevant that it runs counter to the conventional view of tyranny, and the long duration of this tyranny (the hundred years are roughly correct) certainly suggests that it was acceptable to the majority. In detail, Aristotle says that they treated their subjects with moderation; that they mostly subjected themselves to the laws; that Cleisthenes was formidable because of his warlike character; and that they sought the people's favour by taking good care of them. This sounds reasonable enough, except that it is not quite clear what he means by the "laws"—perhaps just that the tyrants tried to conform to existing custom and made their autocracy as inconspicuous as possible[57].

Orthagoras' reign is also like Cypselus' in that no events are recorded from it. Of his successor Myron I we hear that he won an Olympic victory and that he dedicated a great bronze model of a chamber at Olympia (sculpture in bronze was the art at which Sicyonians excelled), but no more[58]. During these quiet reigns Sicyon, overshadowed by her neighbour Corinth, attracts little attention, but as the Corinthian tyranny drew to a close, Sicyon entered on a period of power under the brilliant Cleisthenes, whose reign began in the first decade of the sixth century.

(d) CLEISTHENES

His accession seems to have involved some sort of secondary revolution. Ephorus tells an involved story, how he procured the murder of one of his brothers and the deposition of the other (on the interesting ground that he was plotting with the Cypselids of Corinth), and Aristotle cites the succession of Cleisthenes to Myron II as an example of a revolution which merely replaced one tyranny by another. His distinction means nothing fundamental about the character of Cleisthenes' rule, for the general judgment just cited applies to him as well as to his predecessors. But the new tyranny was in some ways different, and followed a more active policy, while internally Cleisthenes laid emphasis on the racial division inside Sicyon[59].

The evidence for this comes from Herodotus, who tells us that he was at war with Argos and lists the odd forms which his hatred of Argos took. He stopped the recitation of the Homeric poems at Sicyon, because they celebrated the deeds of the Argives. He tried to expel the hero Adrastus, an Argive who in the myth became king of Sicyon, from his shrine in the market-place, where some sort of primitive tragic choruses were performed, of the kind elsewhere associated with the god Dionysus. Cleisthenes asked Delphi's advice about this, and received the rough answer that Adrastus had been king of Sicyon, "but you are a stone-thrower" (whatever this means, it was evidently an insult). Rebuffed here, he tried an oblique method, obtaining from Thebes the bones of Adrastus' legendary enemy Melanippus, for whom he built a shrine and assigned to him most of Adrastus' sacrifices, but the choruses to Dionysus. Thirdly he changed the Dorian tribe-names because they were the same for Sicyon as for Argos, and called them Pigmen, Assmen and Swinemen instead of Hylleis, Pamphyloi and Dymanes, while he gave his own tribe the name Archelaoi, the rulers.

Childish as this is, it must be taken as seriously as the modern campaigns of propaganda of which it is the ancient counter-part. The Spartans were entirely in earnest when in the middle of the sixth century they marked a change in their foreign policy by stealing the bones of Orestes from Arcadia, and Cimon's dis-covery of the bones of Theseus on Scyros in 475 was an event of political importance[60]. The question to determine is whether Cleisthenes' campaign was directed merely at Argos, as Herodotus says, or was also a matter of internal politics at Sicyon. The war with Argos was a reality, and the ban on Homer has little point except as a gesture against Argos. But the change of tribe-names goes further than this, for if Cleisthenes was only trying to whip up feeling against Argos, he should try to rally the Dorians of Sicyon to this cause, whereas the new names, and above all the name "rulers" given to his own tribe, are pointless if he is not asserting the superiority of the non-Dorians. Here then is one tyranny with a racial prejudice. But the symptoms appear some fifty to sixty years after the beginning of the tyranny, and are characteristic of Cleisthenes, not Orthagoras.

Delphi's outspoken rebuke to Cleisthenes in the matter of Adrastus must come at the very beginning of the reign, for about 595 Cleisthenes was taking part in the First Sacred War, after which the oracle's tone was very different. The position of Delphi, and of the religious association called the Amphictiony which had charge of it, is not easy to describe. Delphi was the seat of the infallible oracle of Apollo, a great part of whose business was purely religious, the determination of ritual and such matters.

But the oracle was also asked practical and political questions, and it could not avoid taking part in politics. Sometimes it made mistakes, and inevitably it became itself the object of political manœuvre, even at times of open fighting. The pious, of whom there were many (Herodotus is a conspicuous example), had to accommodate themselves to these facts, and found it possible to do so. It was made easier by the extreme ambiguity of many Delphic responses, and by the circulation of oracles concocted after the event to show that Delphi had always known what was coming: we have seen some examples already.

The First Sacred War took the form of an attack on the city of Crisa in the plain below Delphi, which controlled access to the shrine from the sea, the natural approach from the south and west. The attack was led by the Thessalian Eurylochus and Cleisthenes of Sicyon, and a contingent came from Athens under the leadership of Alcmeon. This is one of several attempts by Thessaly to extend her influence southwards: they were short-lived, mainly because of Thessalian disunion, but Thessaly kept control of many of the minor peoples round the head of the Malian Gulf who made up the Amphictiony of Delphi. Cleisthenes had an insult to avenge, and was no doubt glad to see the destruction of a trading port on the shore opposite Sicyon: his part was the construction of a fleet to cut Crisa off from the sea[61]. Athens was concerned because Delphi some forty years earlier had backed Cylon in his attempt to become tyrant of Athens, and Alcmeon's father Megacles had got into trouble on that occasion (p. 49 and Chapter VII).

Crisa was besieged, taken and destroyed, and to celebrate the victory the festival of the Pythian Apollo at Delphi was reorganized and enlarged: this was in 590, and after some further changes the numbered series of the Pythia begins in 582. Cleisthenes was given a third of the spoils, with which he set up a festival at Sicyon, also called Pythia. (This appears to be not entirely a new festival, but in part the reorganization of one that had been dedicated to Adrastus.) The fact that Delphi was under new management appears in its relations with the tyrants. Before 595 we have seen Delphi friendly to Cypselus and openly rude to Cleisthenes, after 590 we find Delphi hostile to the Corinthian tyranny (p. 48), whereas Cleisthenes competed with success at the Delphic Pythia and built at Delphi a Sicyonian treasury, some of whose sculptures have been found.

Something must also be said of the spectacular meeting about 570 which ended in the marriage of Cleisthenes' daughter Agariste to the Athenian Megacles, the son of Alcmeon[62]. Herodotus tells us about this competition organized in the leisurely style of the epic. A formal invitation was proclaimed at Olympia after Cleisthenes' victory in the games, the illustrious suitors spent a year in various tests at his court, then on the last evening the dancing of the Athenian Hippocleides grew wilder till at last he stood on his head on a table and waggled his legs : Cleisthenes warned him that he had danced away his marriage, but he replied, "Hippocleides doesn't care." This answer, which became a proverb, decided the issue in favour of the other Athenian Megacles, and it has naturally been suspected that the end, if not the whole, of the story has been coloured up as the result of rivalry between the two great Athenian houses concerned. But Cleisthenes was a man capable of carrying through an elaborate pageant with deliberate reminiscences of the epic—the tyrants show the same magnificent extravagance which was shown later by the great princes of the Renaissance. The list of thirteen suitors from twelve cities shows the extent of Cleisthenes' influence. It raises some historical problems, but here it will be enough to note that it includes suitors from the Greek West, but none from the eastern side of the Aegean. Cleisthenes' interests tended westwards, which helps to account for his intervention against Crisa which depended on the western trade. But it was only in special circumstances that Sicyon could become a naval power, hampered as she was by having no good port.

No more great events are recorded from Cleisthenes' reign, and we do not even know how his war with Argos went. But enough has survived to show his power, which was favoured by the decline of Corinth and confirmed by the result of the Sacred War. The tyranny lasted for a while after his death, and was put down by the Spartans in the 550's. Surprisingly, Cleisthenes' tribe-names were not at once abolished—Sparta perhaps did not want to favour the Dorians too openly—but before the end of the century the old Dorian names were restored and the non-Dorian tribe was given the innocuous name Aigialeis.

(e) ELIS, "PISA" AND OLYMPIA

The "Pisatan" tyranny can be dealt with more summarily[63]. It was remembered principally as part of a dispute over the presidency of the Olympic games, which was normally held by Elis. The centre of the Elean state was in the plain called Hollow Elis in the north-west corner of the Peloponnese, the area conquered first and occupied most completely by the invading Eleans. Olympia lies further south, in the valley of the Alpheus, which was conquered later and whose small towns seem to have contained a higher proportion of pre-conquest inhabitants. Still further south lay territory which was attacked by Elis only at the very end of the seventh century and was still capable of resistance in the fifth.

The place where the Olympic festival was held was often called Pisa, but there was no city or separate state of Pisa in historical times. This confusing concept arose out of the quarrels between Elis and Arcadia in the 360's, when it suited Arcadia to say that "Pisa" was the original president and the Eleans were usurpers. The notion took some root, though not exactly in this form: later histories of the festival make Elis found it in 776, but speak of an interlude of Pisatan presidency from 660 to 572 (or dates close to these). But the oldest version of the history of Olympia, compiled by Hippias of Elis about 400 (before the quarrel with Arcadia), seems to have known only of two single interruptions to Elis' presidency, the irregularly held Olympiads of 668 and 588.

This is the background against which our sources occasionally mention the "Pisatan" tyranny of Pantaleon, whose doings were described by Aristotle, and his sons Damophon and Pyrrhus, whose reigns are dated by Pausanias to the early sixth century. There is no doubt that the state of Pisa is a figment, but this is not sufficient reason for denying the historicity of Pantaleon, and we have good enough grounds for supposing that there were quarrels over Olympia in the seventh century: Herodotus says that Pheidon seized the festival, and we can identify this seizure with the irregular celebration of 668 (p. 41). If the tyranny is real, it is most naturally interpreted as a reassertion of their independence by the pre-conquest inhabitants of the Alpheus valley. We need not think of this event as a struggle between two separate states, "Pisa" and Elis. More probably it is a struggle for power within a single state, which was called throughout Elis, though the state and the festival were for a while under the tyrant's control and not in the hands of the normal authority centred in Hollow Elis. In the early sixth century the Eleans of the north conquered the Alpheus valley for good, and the expansion of Elis to the south continued till it met with Sparta's expansion to the west over Messenia.

(f) MESSENIA

The Messenians had very early lost ground to Sparta, and in the late eighth century the Spartan king Theopompus completed the conquest of their territory. In the course of the seventh century there was a formidable revolt, often called the Second Messenian War, which cost Sparta many years and much trouble to suppress. There were later revolts as well, notably the one set off by the great Spartan earthquake of 465, but in general Sparta now held Messenia firmly till it was liberated by the Theban general Epaminondas in the winter of 370/69. After this—indeed the process had begun before—the history of the early wars became a subject for propaganda designed to show that one side or the other was throughout in the wrong, and details were recklessly added. But we can see the outline. The revolt is related to the complex of wars waged between Sparta and Argos in the later seventh century. Sparta and Elis were allies, eager to avenge the defeats they had suffered at the hands of Pheidon and having a common object in the conquest of the western Peloponnese. Arcadia and the "Pisatans" were bound to resist this combination, and the story that they helped Messenia is comparatively early and wholly plausible.

The question is where the Messenians themselves stand in the racial division of the Peloponnese. If they were a Dorian people, as their descendants thought, their alliance in the seventh century with pre-Dorian peoples is perfectly intelligible, for they had their independence to defend: Dorian Argos, with less at stake, was always ready to combine with Arcadian cities against her inveterate enemy, Sparta. In the classical period the Messenians spoke Doric, and the fact that their dialect was indistinguishable from that of their Spartan masters was of use to the Athenian general Demosthenes in the Peloponnesian War of the late fifth century when he organized raids by Messenian parties in Spartan territory. Already in the fifth century the Messenians have a place in the Dorian legend of the return of the Heraclidae and their division of the Peloponnese (p. 54)[64].

On the other hand, in spite of the Dorian legend, their early kings have connections with Arcadia, and the dynasty bears the Arcadian name Aipytidai. Further, and this is important as the only piece of evidence older than the eighth-century Spartan conquest, the Corinthian poet Eumelus (p. 44) wrote for them in the days of their independence a processional hymn for their sacred embassy to Delos, and Delos is an Ionian sanctuary where a Dorian embassy would be very much out of place. Finally the Spartan poet Tyrtaeus, in the difficult days of the Second Messenian War, comforts his countrymen by saying that they are the "race of unconquered Heracles" and Zeus will therefore not allow them to be defeated. This is wartime feeling, against an enemy whom the Spartans had already once reduced to slavery, but Tyrtaeus could hardly write like this if it was generally believed that the Messenians were also descended from the great Dorian hero and were of the same race as the Spartans[65].

The early Messenians may thus have been less Dorian than was imagined in the fifth century, but the question is hardly to be solved with our present evidence: future excavation in Messenia may help to answer it. If they were not Dorians, we should have to suppose that their incorporation into the Dorian legend took place later, when their dialect had become firmly Doric, in some centre where there were free Messenians in the classical period. A likely quarter would be Rhegium, where there were old and influential families of Messenian origin, and Messana across the strait in Sicily, where Doric was spoken and some Messenian refugees were settled early in the fifth century[66].

(g) CONCLUSION

The racial division of the Peloponnese was still remembered and felt in the classical period, and it may be presumed that it was more strongly felt in the seventh century. But the attempt to examine it reveals the limitation of our knowledge. Since the only persons of whom we hear even the names are the tyrants themselves, we are ignorant of the social structure of the tyrannies, and have to rely very much on general impressions.

The racial question affected only people of the social class represented roughly by Aëtion, and the admission of such people to political privilege was carried through in Corinth and Sicyon without much trouble. If there had been a general movement for the liberation of serfs in the Dorian states (p. 55), a much stronger racial feeling would have been generated, and the whole affair would have left very different traces in the record. As it is, we hear nothing of anti-Dorian feeling at Corinth, and at Sicyon it does not appear until Cleisthenes' accession about 600.

What caused this outbreak in Sicyon we can only guess. The tyranny seems to have been in difficulties at the time (p. 58), and it may be that the new tyrant could no longer reckon on quiet and general support from the citizens, but had to whip up sectional feeling against the Dorians, and national feeling against Argos and perhaps Corinth too. In the south it seems clear that resistance to Spartan aggression is a more substantial motive than pure racial feeling. Only in Elis could we suppose that this feeling was the main cause of a tyranny, but Elis is the state about which we know least of all.

The general conclusion seems to be that tension between the races in the Peloponnese existed and was a real factor in the discontent of the time, but was a secondary factor which did not by itself decide any issue. Elsewhere the problem does not arise in the same form. In Athens, where there was a tyranny, there was no consciousness of racial division, in Thessaly where conquerors and conquered were very much aware of division there was no tyranny.

THE SPARTAN ALTERNATIVE TO TYRANNY

THE Spartan system, which was not merely a political constitution but a general way of life, was a standing wonder to the
Greeks, admired but not imitated, an inspiration to political
theorists and a comfort to those who found democracy distasteful.
The achievements of Sparta compelled admiration. In an unstable
world, her constitution remained unchanged for centuries, and
she had no tyrant before the end of the third century. The power
which she had built up during the sixth century was the nucleus
of Greek resistance to Persia in 480, and it was the growth of this
power, and the steadfastness displayed by Leonidas and his men
at Thermopylae, that impelled Herodotus to make the earliest
surviving attempt to describe the Spartan system. Sparta in the
end defeated Athens in the great struggle of the Peloponnesian
War in the late fifth century, and among the generation which
witnessed this defeat there were those who drew the moral that
Spartan oligarchy must be right and Athenian democracy a
mistake. There was criticism of Sparta, notably from Thucydides
and Aristotle, but it became nevertheless an accepted doctrine
that the Spartan system was an admirable instrument forged by a
great lawgiver to inculcate in the citizens the virtues of courage
and political concord.

The system was supposed to have been laid down by Lycurgus
at a very early date—most ancient estimates point to the ninth
century, well outside our normal historical range. The legend of
this Lycurgus, and the Greek belief that the whole system was
created at a single stroke, are substantially unhistorical and
obstruct enquiry. It is therefore necessary to begin by reviewing
the institutions ascribed to Lycurgus and discussing their claims
to an early date: the historical development of Sparta cannot
be described until the ground has been cleared[67].

(a) THE LYCURGAN SYSTEM

(i) A complicated social code governed the whole life of the citizens, and more particularly their training in youth. The state took charge of a boy at seven, and from fourteen to twenty-one youths were grouped in age-classes with strange archaic names[68], and trained under strict supervision. The adult males took their meals together in messes called *syssitia*, and in general home life was cut down and the sexes separated to an extent which other Greeks thought remarkable. Similar customs existed in the cities of Crete, and it was disputed in antiquity where they had originated and which had copied from the other. The special feature of the Spartan version was the strict equality maintained among the citizens. Sparta prided herself on her social as well as her military discipline, and the respect accorded to age, authority and tradition.

(ii) Allied to this are certain rules of a partly sumptuary, partly economic nature like the enactment that axe and saw were the only tools to be used on the materials from which a Spartan's house was built. Frugality, and a blunt wit at the expense of unnecessary luxury, were recognized Spartan virtues, and frugality was needed to maintain the appearance of equality. The only rule of serious economic importance which is attributed to Lycurgus is the prohibition of silver coinage to private citizens. In its place Sparta retained the cumbrous archaic currency of iron "spits" which had been used in many parts of mainland Greece before the introduction of silver currency in the late seventh century (Chapter VII).

(iii) Lycurgus was also credited with a redistribution of land, into equal lots for each citizen. In practice, land was not equally divided in any period known to us, but there was a distinction between two classes of Spartan land, to be discussed presently, which may be relevant to this question.

(iv) The army which made Sparta for two centuries the most formidable power in Greece was naturally reckoned as the creation of Lycurgus. Herodotus mentions his military institutions and makes the Lycurgan reform generally the cause of

Sparta's rise in the sixth century, but gives no systematic account. Xenophon describes with more precision the army of the early fourth century, and makes Lycurgus responsible for every detail[69].

(v) The political constitution was also ascribed as a whole to Lycurgus, except for the double kingship, an institution clearly earlier than his reputed date. In classical Sparta sovereignty resided in the assembly, in the sense that its vote gave the final decision on important questions, and the rights of this assembly were guaranteed by the archaic document known as the Great Rhetra, quoted by Plutarch in his *Life of Lycurgus*[70]. Rhetra appears to mean an enactment of the state, and the Great Rhetra, after referring to the founding of certain temples, the division of the people into tribes and "*obai*", and the establishment of a council of elders (the Gerousia) of thirty members including the two kings, then lays down the procedure for legislation at Sparta— there are to be regular meetings of the assembly, proposals are to be put before it by the Gerousia, the decision on these proposals lies with the people (*demos*). In a rider which is said to have been added later the sovereignty of the assembly is slightly limited: if the people go astray, the kings and council may stop the proceedings. The point of this is said to be that the people had taken to altering, by excessive amendment, the whole sense of the proposals laid before them, and the rider gives the council a veto in such cases. Only one other feature of the constitution calls for mention here, the powerful magistracy of the five ephors who are the main executive of the state, and are sometimes said to have been set up by Lycurgus, sometimes to have been added a century or more after his time.

(b) ORIGINS OF PARTICULAR INSTITUTIONS

It is at first sight unlikely that all these institutions date from the same period: the social system outlined in para. (i) has a very primitive air, but the highly efficient army of classical Sparta can hardly have retained its organization unchanged through the centuries. A closer examination confirms this impression.

(i) The training of the youth, the communal meals, the

segregation of the sexes attracted most attention in the fourth century. It was these features that occasioned the dispute over the priority of Spartan and Cretan institutions: the land law and political constitutions of Crete and Sparta were not so obviously allied, as was seen by the hard-headed historian Polybius in the second century, criticizing the writings of his predecessors on the subject[71], and by themselves they would not have suggested that one state was dependent on the other. But it is precisely the social features of the two systems which anthropologists find most familiar, and similar institutions occur among many warlike races at a certain stage of their development all over the world. There is no question of Crete copying Sparta or Sparta Crete. Both inherited these institutions from an earlier phase in the development of the Dorian race, before that race split up into the separate Dorian states of Greek history.

The peculiarity of Sparta and Crete is that they kept these institutions up for so long after others had discarded them. The remoteness of Crete from the main stream of classical Greek history may account for their survival there. In Sparta it is possible that they were deliberately retained, or even tightened up, in the interests of military training—the Spartan version is stricter than the Cretan—and it is here that we might look for the hand of a legislator. But the origins of the system lie further back than any date ever assigned to Lycurgus.

(ii) The austerity of classical Sparta, which was taken to be a deliberate feature of the Lycurgan dispensation, appears to date only from the beginning of the fifth century, or very little earlier. The evidence of excavation and the fragments of the seventh-century poet Alcman alike show that the course of her cultural development was quite normal down into the sixth century, and bear witness to a gaiety and charm in archaic Sparta which could not have been guessed from the writings of the fourth century. Laconian pottery is an attractive fabric, not the equal of Corinth's best, but an individual style which is at its best in the second quarter of the sixth century, and then declines in much the same manner as all other Greek fabrics except Attic. Laconian craftsmen also excelled in the carving of ivory and in bronze-work[72].

No interruption is to be detected in the development of

these arts, except that from a date about 600 imports into Laconia virtually cease, a consequence which has been referred to Sparta's retention of an iron currency at the time when other states were taking to silver. The maintenance of this obsolete medium must be a deliberate act of state, but this does not mean that the whole Lycurgan system must be dated as late as 600 : the prohibition of silver currency could not occur till silver currency was invented.

But the general character of archaic Spartan civilization is of some negative importance to our judgment of the system. It means that one conspicuous feature of the life of classical "Lycurgan" Sparta was not present in the seventh century, and if any reform was carried out in the seventh or early sixth centuries it did not immediately affect the quality of the objects made for Spartan citizens by Laconian craftsmen. The fact that Alcman's poems, for all their local colour and personal character, are so very much poems of their time shows that Sparta in his day was not a state set apart from the rest.

(iii) Redivision of land was a standing demand of Greek revolutionaries, and the Greeks in general tended to imagine an ideal past when land had been equally divided. Statements about this ideal past must always be treated with reserve, and in Sparta there is the further complication that the details of the scheme attributed to Lycurgus have been affected by the propaganda and activities of the revolutionary kings of the third century, Agis IV and Cleomenes III, who attempted a redivision of land, claiming of course that their only purpose was to restore the system of Lycurgus.

But before their time there was a distinction, known to Aristotle in the fourth century, between two types of Spartan land, one of which could legally be sold though convention frowned on sale, while the other, the "original allotment", was inalienable by law[73]. Whatever the actual origin of this distinction, the owner of such an "original allotment" no doubt thought of it as the piece of land assigned to his ancestor by Lycurgus, but that does not help us to date the assignment. Aristotle found evidence in a poem of Tyrtaeus that there was an agitation for the redistribution of land as a result of hardships caused by the Second Messenian War[74], but we do not know if any redistribution was carried out then. The most that can be said is that if any redistribution had taken place later than the middle of the sixth century we should almost certainly have heard of it.

The relevance of this to the classical Spartan system lies in the fact that the formal qualification for citizenship was the citizen's continuing ability to contribute his share in kind to the common meal of his *syssition*[75], and that the efficiency of the army depended on the soldier being economically independent and free to devote his time to military training, so that if he lost his land the state lost both a citizen and a soldier. It was therefore natural for Sparta to discourage the alienation of land, and essential at the beginning, when the system was first set up, that there should be enough citizens in possession of a reasonable minimum of land.

(iv) We can distinguish at least three phases in the development of the Spartan army. Hoplite armour and tactics (Chapter III) were introduced at the beginning of the seventh century. We do not know in detail how the army was then organized, but we get some light from a papyrus fragment of Tyrtaeus, the lines of which are so broken that no continuous reconstruction of the poem is possible, but they contain at one point an unmistakable reference to the three Dorian tribes (p. 13) fighting as separate units. This has usually, and rightly, been taken to mean that the organization of the army in three regiments based on the original tribes of kinship survived into the seventh century[76].

The next distinguishable phase is one in which the army had five main units called *lochoi*. Aristotle gives us their names: the rest are unintelligible to us, but one called Mesoates is clearly named from Mesoa, one of the four "villages" which made up the city of Sparta. Presumably then three of the others, though they bear fancy names, belong to the other three "villages": the remaining one will then most probably belong to the town of Amyclae a few miles south of Sparta. These are local, not racial, divisions, and they seem to be the divisions called *obai* in the Rhetra (p. 68), each *oba* providing one *lochos*. If that is so, we get some indication of the stage of Spartan development to which the Rhetra belongs. It was the army of the five *lochoi* which fought the Persians at Plataea in 479, supported by an equal number of *perioikoi*, the free but voteless inhabitants of the other towns of Laconia[77].

A further change took place before the end of the fifth century, and the army described by Thucydides and again more precisely by Xenophon was organized in six units called *morai*. Spartans and *perioikoi* no longer now fought in separate units, but were incorporated together in the subdivisions of the *morai*[78].

None of this can have anything to do with a lawgiver of the ninth century. The army of Xenophon's day was not a copy of the archaic army, nor even of the army that fought in the Persian Wars, but the result of a fifth-century reorganization. The truth is evidently that each Spartan generation liked to think that the current organization of the army had the sanction of antiquity and of the name of Lycurgus.

(v) In politics we may expect the same tendency, to ascribe to Lycurgus the whole of the current constitution and practice of Sparta. The Great Rhetra (the central point of the flourishing modern controversy . over the Spartan constitution) was inevitably supposed to be Lycurgus' work, but in view of what we have just seen in other departments of Spartan life we need not take this too seriously and must examine the Rhetra on its merits.

It is important to realize that the procedure of council and assembly laid down in the Rhetra is not peculiar to Sparta or at all eccentric for a Greek state. It is a version of the probouleutic system common throughout Greece (p. 14–15), and the main principle, that proposals should be initiated by a council and voted on by an assembly, is the regular method of settling important questions in classical times in Sparta, Athens or almost any city.

The assembly at Sparta was a narrow body by Athenian standards. The *perioikoi* who lived in the other towns of Laconia, free but without a voice in the policy of the state and liable for service in wars about which they were not consulted, would have been voters in Attica. On the other hand, this assembly included all the citizen hoplites and numbered some thousands, so that it was a wide enough body by the standards of any classical oligarchy, and numerous in comparison with the aristocratic bodies which had the effective government of Greek cities in the eighth and early seventh centuries.

The Gerousia of thirty members was a small council by Athenian standards, and alien to democratic principles in that its members were appointed for life. When fourth-century writers discuss the political constitution of Sparta they often pick on the Gerousia as the characteristically Lycurgan feature, probably because no other prominent city of their time still had an effective aristocratic council of this type. For the seventh century it would not be abnormal. At that time the Athenian Areopagus, composed of life members, was the main organ of Athenian government, and we hear of similar councils in Elis, Crete and elsewhere.

The Rhetra thus exemplifies a form of government normal to Greece, but in an oligarchic rather than a democratic version. Another oligarchic feature is the wide latitude given to the executive, the kings and ephors, compared with the restrictions put upon archons and generals at Athens. The composition of the Gerousia seems to show further that Sparta had a somewhat archaic version of the usual pattern. Probably then the constitution at Sparta received a fixed form at a date comparatively early for a Greek city. Another indication of this is the retention of hereditary kings as active officers of state, a feature not found in the constitutions of other cities.

A rough date for the Rhetra can be gained from the fact that the assembly was composed of hoplites, which means that it cannot be earlier than the introduction of hoplites soon after 700. On the other hand, some verses of Tyrtaeus[79] paraphrase an oracle roughly identical in content with the Rhetra, which is therefore not later than Tyrtaeus' lifetime. The organization of the army by tribes of kinship lasted into the time of Tyrtaeus, or near it, whereas the *obai*, which are based on locality, are referred to in the Rhetra. This too points to the lifetime of Tyrtaeus.

Further, the fact that the Rhetra is recorded at all is significant. Sparta disapproved of written laws, indeed Lycurgus is said to have forbidden them, and the Rhetra would not have been preserved unless its contents were important and had been the subject of controversy. The fact that the hoplites were called *homoioi*, the "equals", shows that there had been inequality before the settlement. The rights of the hoplite *demos* were new, and had been gained, not without struggle, from a narrower aristocracy. We may recall that Aristotle found in Tyrtaeus evidence that there had been discontent in Sparta at the time of the Second Messenian War, and, more generally, that the seventh century was a period when there were violent revolutions in other cities. The answer to the problem of the Rhetra seems therefore to be that it was the settlement of political trouble at Sparta at the time when tyrants were being set up elsewhere. The significance of this result for the general question of tyranny has been pointed out in an earlier chapter (p. 37).

(c) THE DEVELOPMENT OF THE SPARTAN CONSTITUTION

We have now reached a point where something like narrative can be attempted. Using the results of the previous discussion, and inclining wherever there is a choice to the view that the early development of Sparta was comparatively normal, the main lines seem to be as follows.

The origins of the double kingship, hereditary in the two separate families Agiadae and Eurypontidae, lie too far back for our guesses about them to find much confirmation. The magistracy of the ephors is a later creation. A list of the heads of this annual college was preserved at Sparta, and is reported to have reached back to the year 754[80], that is, well into the period when aristocratic government might be expected in a Greek city. It is natural to suppose that this magistracy arose, like others elsewhere, from the successful effort of the nobles to limit the powers of the kings. In that case the oath sworn every month between the kings and ephors (p. 11) witnesses an early bargain between aristocracy and monarchy, perhaps the bargain by which the ephorate itself was set up. Sparta is unusual in that the kingship retained its hereditary character, so that the kings and ephors became independent and even rival authorities, a situation that did not arise where the king was reduced to an annual magistrate.

In the eighth century the old-style army under king Theopompus completed the conquest of Messenia. At the beginning of the seventh the hoplite army was introduced, with Sparta still bent on expansion, to the east as well as to the west, but in 669 she was heavily defeated by Argos at Hysiae (p. 40), and she seems thereafter for a while to have given up ideas of conquest. At this time Sparta was still open to the economic influences which affected other Greek states, though she showed no signs of becoming a commercial city in the style of Corinth. In the middle of the seventh century or a little later she was involved with Argos, Arcadia and Elis in a complex of local wars, and also in a major Messenian revolt. To judge by the length of this Second Messenian War and by the strictures of Tyrtaeus, the Spartan army did not at first distinguish itself. These setbacks brought aristocratic government into discredit, as similar troubles did at Corinth (p. 44), and hardship caused by the war led to agitation for redistribution of land. Sparta was ripe for tyranny.

Instead she underwent a reform of her old institutions. The army was reorganized and units based on locality took the place of tribal units based on descent. The numbers and composition of the council were fixed, and the composition and powers of the assembly whose members are hereafter called "equals" : a council will certainly have existed before and probably some sort of assembly, but the Rhetra made their relation to one another definite and regular. It may be that at this time the old social institutions of Dorian Sparta were furbished up and directed consciously towards military training. It must remain uncertain whether there was any redistribution of land, on a large or a small scale : nor can we be sure whether the prohibition of the sale of one class of holding dates from this time, though it is clear that it would be useful as a safeguard of the new order. Some ancient writers speak of the admission of new citizens after the Second Messenian War, but they tend to confuse the sequels of the First and Second Wars, and in any case the expression has not very much meaning if the precise limits of the citizen body were only at this stage being fixed.

This reform must have been carefully and deliberately planned. In the second generation of the hoplite army's existence, Spartan statesmen saw that the aristocratic monopoly of government was doomed, and being warned by the example of revolution at Corinth and elsewhere, they preferred to proceed by the way of peaceful reform. So they gave Sparta the first hoplite constitution of Greek history. They were ahead of their time, but completely successful in their remedy for revolution, and their military reforms coupled with their new political solution gave Sparta the lead which she enjoyed in the sixth century. But the constitution which was liberal and progressive when it was defined in the Rhetra in the seventh century seemed archaic and reactionary to the democrats of the fifth. Nevertheless, it had served so well that the Spartans were unable either to abandon it or to remodel it again—to make it more liberal would have meant abandoning their absolute dominion over the rest of Laconia—and that is the basis of Sparta's later conservatism.

(d) LYCURGUS

The shadow of the lawgiver deserves a note at the end of the chapter. At the beginning it was stated, and it has been argued in detail since, that the legend of Lycurgus was an obstacle to enquiry, but it may reasonably be asked who he was and why the Spartans thought him so important that they ascribed everything to him and nothing to any other reformer.

He can be no more than a shadow to us, because in the early stages of the growth of the legend he was little more to his countrymen. When they first decided to set up a shrine to him, they had to ask Delphi for a ruling whether he was a god or a man, and this shows that he was not at that time, whenever it was, a recent and familiar figure. His name did not occur in either of the royal pedigrees : Simonides and Herodotus in the fifth century, and all other writers thereafter, make him uncle and regent to an infant king. This was a device to account for his authority, not genuine family tradition, for Herodotus makes him uncle to an Agiad king, but Simonides and the rest make him Eurypontid. Nevertheless, uncertain as they were about his personality, the Spartans did decide to set up a shrine and a cult to Lycurgus[81].

The most plausible explanation is that Lycurgus was already a name, but not much more, in Spartan tradition when the crisis occurred in the seventh century, and that the reformers represented their reforms as the restoration of the neglected laws of this Lycurgus. This will account for the fact that no name of any seventh-century reformer is preserved. It involves some conscious deception, and in particular it looks as if the oracle paraphrased by Tyrtaeus (p. 73) must have been a forgery. Such deceptions have prospered on other occasions, and this was wholly successful. The dim, remote lawgiver, once his cult was established, acquired more definite outline; by the fourth century his position in the

Eurypontid family was fixed; historians and biographers added more and more detail, till when Plutarch came to write his life in the second century A.D. there was a wealth of accepted "fact" to describe and comment on. But if there was a real Lycurgus, we know nothing of him.

CHAPTER VII

THE ECONOMIC FACTOR: SOLON OF ATHENS

THE condition of Attica at the time of Solon's appointment as archon[82] in 594 illustrates the dislocation which might take place, during a time of rising prosperity, in a society not yet fully accustomed to the use of coinage. The immediate and urgent problem arose from the hardship caused to small landowners by the current law of debt, and Solon's immediate remedy was a cancellation of existing debts and a reform of the law for the future. This can be regarded as a separate operation only partly connected with the main body of his political and constitutional reforms: these were of more permanent importance for the development of Athens, but we must look first at the economic factor, the discussion of which was postponed in an earlier chapter (p. 31), and see how the conditions of the time came to bear so hardly on the Attic farmer.

(a) COMMERCE AND COLONIZATION

The growing prosperity of Greece was a necessary condition of the developments described in previous chapters. Hoplite armies were made possible by the fact that individuals were rich enough to provide themselves with hoplite equipment. Trade with Sicily, Italy and North-west Greece was an essential part of the history of both Bacchiad and Cypselid Corinth. So too were the colonies which Corinth planted on the main routes of this trade.

Greek colonies, however, were not mere trading posts, but substantive cities, needing land for a predominantly agricultural population. The Greek peninsula itself is a hard land for farmers, and its limited crops will not by themselves support a large population. In the dark ages of Greek history the country was poor and relatively empty, as the material remains of the tenth century show[83], but by 750 there were already too many mouths to feed, and in the following centuries the Greeks poured out over the ancient world as colonists, traders and mercenaries, first on their own initiative and then in the wake of Alexander's conquests, till eventually in the second century the homeland began to suffer again from under-population.

In the eighth century, when this pressure of population first showed itself, the colonies offered a direct escape from overcrowded land, and land was the object of most of the colonists who, in the years following 735, founded city after city in East Sicily and South Italy. This is evidently true of the Chalcidian foundations of Leontini and Catana which shared the fertile plain of North-east Sicily, and of the Achaeans who settled and throve in South Italy. But it is not the whole truth about Corinthian Corcyra, whose position on the route from Greece to Italy must always have been an important consideration, nor about the Chalcidian cities of Rhegium and Zancle which commanded, and were founded to command, the Straits of Messina. The Euboeans who founded Cumae in the Bay of Naples, the earliest colony in the West, passed by many sites more eligible for agriculturalists, and the position of their remote settlement suggests that they were after Etruscan metal. Another very early colony, Milesian Sinope on the south shore of the Black Sea, was planted near mines which were the oldest source of iron known to the Greeks. Another was the Ionian settlement at Posideion (Al Mina) at the mouth of the Orontes, which opened up Greek trade with Syria and Mesopotamia, not in corn but in the manufactures of those older civilizations[84].

Trade and colonization may be distinguished in this earliest phase of Greek expansion, but they were not separate in practice. Overseas trade began a little earlier than the main stream of agricultural emigration, and it was through traders that the Greeks learnt of the agricultural sites that were open to them in other lands. The colonists established new Greek cities abroad on the model of their cities at home: the movement relieved, though it did not abolish, the overcrowding of the home country, and many of the new cities had a corn surplus for export. But the traders who began this expansion and influenced the siting of some early colonies were not always or mainly concerned with the food supply. Greece was also poor in many raw materials, notably in metal, and much of the trade was in manufactured articles, which enriched the lives of the Greek upper classes and led to further demands for the trader and the manufacturer to satisfy.

The question for us is the effect of this expansion on the Greeks at home. The small farmer who did not emigrate had still a hard struggle to gain his livelihood. The Greek manufacturer, stimulated by the Oriental models now made known to him and to his customers, prospered and exported his wares to Greek colonists and foreigners alike (our evidence is chiefly the pottery, which has survived while textiles and metalwork have perished). Manufacturers and traders, grown rich, had leisure to become ambitious too and impatient of aristocratic monopoly. The nobles themselves, wealthy already by Greek standards, acquired new appetites, a new use for their wealth, and an incentive to increase it.

The wealthy noble and the wealthy commoner were divided by the criterion of birth, and so by the privilege which in the early seventh century still automatically accompanied good birth, but there was no other gulf between them. Greece did not develop a separate class of merchants, with feelings and ideals of its own. The nobles themselves were quick to seize the opportunities which the age offered: the Bacchiadae exploited Corinth's growing trade, and the two great eighth-century colonies had noble founders (p. 44). Other aristocracies will have done the like, in proportion to the resources of their cities. But in this new trade, as in the new style of warfare, the nobles could not exercise a monopoly. We can detect at Athens, and must assume at Corinth and elsewhere, a considerable class of men outside the circle of the well-born, who felt that their wealth qualified them for privilege. They were, or readily became, landowners (when Solon broke the aristocratic monopoly his new criterion was income in kind from the land) and were assimilated to the governing class. Aristocratic poets might complain, like Theognis, that nobility was diluted by marriage with mere wealth, but the dilution went on in spite of the protest[85].

Thus one main result of the economic expansion which began around 750 was to create in the course of time groups of wealthy men, not radically different in habits or feeling from the nobility, who must increasingly have felt that their exclusion from political privilege was arbitrary and unreasonable, and that it could be terminated. They played their part, no doubt, in the seventh-century revolutions at Corinth and elsewhere, but we see their part more clearly in the constitutional reforms of Solon, to be described in a later section of this chapter. A secondary result was to depress the small farmer. The land was still crowded, and the farmer gained less than others by commerce. As usually happens in periods of economic expansion, the new wealth was very unequally distributed, and the wealthy had a new incentive to exploit all those whose economic position was weaker than their own. Both these processes were intensified by the adoption of silver currency.

(b) COINAGE

When Hesiod wrote his farmer's calendar, the *Works and Days*, Greek commerce had already begun to spread but did not yet use coined money. The precious metals are not at all rare in the world described by Homer, and are highly valued, but when the arms of Glaucus and Diomede are compared in the *Iliad* their value is reckoned in terms of oxen, and when Hesiod speaks of the accumulation of wealth he expresses it by saying that you will have more corn in your barn than other people. The Greeks of this time traded by barter, and even the concept of cattle as currency does not seem to make much headway: it does not reappear in Hesiod[86].

Meanwhile Greek traders increased their contact with eastern nations whose commerce had long been highly developed, and who included the precious metals among their means of exchange: but though these eastern states sometimes guaranteed the quality of the metal, they did not issue fixed units of it, and the traders weighed it out *ad hoc*. On the other hand, the Greeks themselves sporadically used a kind of currency of iron objects, tripods or cups or axes, which must where they were used have been treated as equal units. The best known of these currencies consisted of iron "spits" and gave to the later coinage of mainland Greece the names of its small denominations, obol (spit) and drachma (handful, of six spits)[87]. The final step to true coinage was taken among the Lydians and Ionian Greeks of Asia Minor in the third quarter of the seventh century, when first private traders, and then very quickly the state, began to issue pieces whose stamp was a guarantee both of quality and of quantity. The first coins of old Greece were struck at Aegina in the last quarter of the century, 625–600[88].

The convenience of this new invention is attested by its continuous use ever since the seventh century, and it is a valuable chronological landmark because the earliest coins can be dated with fair precision by their style and by the objects which accompany the earliest known deposit of true coins, under the base of the cult statue in the Artemisium of Ephesus. But the basic economic change, that is, the change from barter to the use of precious metal as a standard of value, is less easily traced and may perhaps come a little earlier than the introduction of true coinage.

The primary effect of this change was to make it easier to store wealth and to move it about. Hesiod lived in a world of barter, where values were measured directly, one sort of goods against another. In such a world there were practical limits to the accumulation of wealth as Hesiod envisages it, in kind, and though debt was a serious matter among Hesiod's farmers, there were limits to that too. When wealth began to be measured in the compact and imperishable medium of silver, these limits were removed. The wealthy could store up all the silver they could amass for as long as they liked, and it became both easier and more disastrous for the poor to borrow. The change from barter widened the gap between the rich and the poor.

The change is to be placed somewhere between the time of Hesiod, whose *Works and Days* seem to have been written at the end of the eighth century, and the introduction of true coinage in the second half of the seventh. When Hesiod wrote that "wealth is the very life of wretched men", he used the word (*chremata*) which later meant money, but to him meant only goods. At the beginning of the sixth century Alcaeus uses the same word in its new sense when he quotes, as an established proverb, "money makes the man"[89]. The theme can hardly have been new: it was always true, to continue Alcaeus' sentence, that "the poor man has neither rank nor honour", and we need not suppose that Greek aristocrats at any time were specially merciful to impoverished members of their own class. But Alcaeus, his contemporary Solon, and a little later Theognis of Megara, seem to be unusually preoccupied with problems of wealth and poverty, and their preoccupation is a sign of the times.

(c) ATHENS BEFORE SOLON

The economic and political development of Athens in the century before Solon had been slow compared with that of Corinth and some other cities. At an earlier stage Athens had held a leading position in Greece, in the ninth and early eighth centuries, before the beginnings of authentic history, when our main guide to the activities of the different states is the character and distribution of their individual styles of Geometric pottery. Attic Geometric was the finest in Greece, exported widely though in small quantity, and from the pictures of sea-fights on the later of these pots it has reasonably been deduced that she was then a naval power. In the latter part of the eighth century the lead passed to Corinth, in naval construction (p. 44), colonization, commerce, pottery and much else. There is nothing from Athens in the first half of the seventh century to compare with Protocorinthian pottery, she founded no colonies then, and her navy seems to have suffered a heavy defeat at the hands of Aegina in the time of king Pheidon of Argos. Her exports and imports shrink, and Aegina, where a great deal of Protoattic pottery has been found, seems to have been her main link with the outside world[90].

Yet it would not be fair to call Athens merely backward. Her painters absorb the new oriental influences at first with undisciplined exuberance, but they steadily gain in sobriety and self-confidence, till by the last quarter of the seventh century it can fairly be said that Attic and Corinthian pottery are on a level, and Attic holds more promise for the future. Though Athens' commerce developed more slowly than Corinth's, her nobles were not poor and the resources of her large territory were not negligible. By the end of the century Athens had revived and was no longer so dependent on Aegina.

Politically there is not much to relate. The families called
Eupatridae who formed the Attic aristocracy were a less narrow
circle than the Bacchiad clan at Corinth, but their monopoly
was not less complete. The first attempt at an Athenian tyranny
was made, about 632, by Cylon who had married the daughter
of the Megarian tyrant Theagenes, but when Cylon seized the
Acropolis with Megarian help there was no general rising, and
the people supported Megacles the Eupatrid archon. We know so
little of Cylon that we cannot say how far his failure was due to his
personal qualities, or to dislike of the support he had from
Athens' enemy Megara, but it is evident that Athens had not yet
reached a point where it was felt that any alternative was prefer-
able to the continuance of aristocratic government. It is also
evident that conditions at Athens were disturbed: Megacles'
massacre of the supporters of Cylon provoked violent feeling,
and remained for long a standing charge against his family, the
Alcmeonidae[91].

A little later, about 625, a written law-code was drawn up
by Dracon[92]. It was an advance that the law should be published at
all, not merely enunciated orally by Eupatrid judges, but Dracon's
code has the reputation of having been extremely harsh, and it is
evident that in Solon's time the law of debt in particular bore
very hard on the poor. There was also an intermittent war with
Megara over the possession of the island of Salamis[93]. But it was
mainly debt and agrarian distress that threatened Athens with
revolution when in 594 Solon, who had already publicized his views
in verse, was appointed archon and mediator.

(d) SOLON AND THE AGRARIAN PROBLEM

Solon was a man of good birth and moderate means, interested
in trade, a self-confident politician of some standing, averse from
extreme remedies. In the crisis which called him to power there
is no doubt that he stands on the side of the poor. Aristotle, who
had read the poems complete, says that he everywhere laid the
blame for Athens' troubles on the rich, and fragments survive
from poems written before his archonship in which he speaks
of himself and the poor in the first person and threatens the rich

in the second—"you who have sated yourselves with good things must keep your proud mind in bounds : for we will not endure it, nor will all be well with you". Long passages are quoted by Demosthenes from a poem which begins by asserting proudly that the city under Athena's protection will never be destroyed, and then complains that wicked citizens are threatening to wreck it. The wreckers are described as "leaders of the people" (*demos* here is the whole nation) and are attacked for their greed and rapacity, which have brought the city to a state of slavery "which is rousing up civil strife and sleeping war" : many of the poor have already been sold abroad. His remedy is a reform of the law which will restrain the unjust and heal the division in the city. To revert to a problem considered earlier, he certainly thought that the nobles, the existing governing class, were guilty of the rapacity he condemns.

Solon, then, came forward primarily as the champion of the poor against their oppressors. As for the other side, he was a man of their own class and he was known not to be a revolutionary extremist : Aristotle says that the upper classes expected him to bring in no far-reaching reform. Solon's own claim, in a later poem, is that he saved "those who held power and were admired for their wealth" from the fate that they would have suffered in a revolution.

The nature of the problem is indicated in general terms in the poem quoted above—the poor had been reduced to a state of virtual, in some cases actual, slavery : the root of the trouble was a harsh law, which might be amended. Fresh light comes from another Solonian poem, and from fourth-century prose accounts of his action. The history of this early period was not committed to writing till nearly two hundred years later, by Hellanicus of Lesbos and by the Athenian local historians of the fourth century[94]. Besides oral tradition, they had the help of Solon's poems and laws, valuable checks but not full materials for a narrative. Somewhere they found the name *hektemoroi* for the class which Solon liberated, and their explanations of the term appear in literature which has survived—Aristotle, whose sketch of Solon is one of the most valuable parts of his *Constitution of Athens*, based on close study of the poems as well as on the local historians ; Plutarch, whose life of Solon uses the local historians among other sources; and the late lexicographers who copied out earlier explanations of unfamiliar terms.

These authorities are not unanimous, but the central fact is clear enough. The *hektemoroi*, in return for a loan or other help from some richer landowner, had contracted to hand over to him one sixth (*hektemorion*) of the produce of the land they tilled, and if they failed in their obligation they and their families became his slaves. Writing after he had laid down office, Solon sums up his achievements and gives pride of place to the claim that he had set the land free by plucking up the *horoi* that everywhere were planted in it. *Horoi* on the land are either boundary-stones (but that will not fit here) or the markers of some transaction like mortgage: in this case they must mark the fact of the obligation of the *hektemoroi*, and the plucking up cancelled the obligation.

This was the Seisachtheia, or "shaking off of burdens", Solon's first great measure of liberation, which freed the farmer already entangled and reformed the law for the future. The transaction by which the *hektemoroi* bound themselves was lawful before 594—indeed the uniform obligation of one sixth might suggest that the form was actually prescribed in Dracon's code—but hereafter it was forbidden to secure loans on the personal freedom of the debtor. The status of *hektemoroi* was abolished and the word itself became obsolete, needing commentary by the fourth century. Solon also describes how he brought bakc men who had been sold in slavery abroad, as well as freeing those enslaved at home.

In other directions we see him trying to strengthen Athens' economic position. He restricted the grant of citizenship to certain categories, including craftsmen who migrated to Athens with their whole families, and Plutarch says that this negative enactment had a positive purpose, to encourage genuine and permanent immigrants: we can trace them in one important industry, for some Corinthian potters migrated[95], and in the course of the sixth century Athens drove all other cities out of the pottery market, helped by the quality of her clay. Solon also prohibited the export of agricultural products except oil, not only to keep home-grown corn at home but to stimulate the oil trade. He instituted the first Attic coinage, on a system which differs in detail from other Greek systems, but the standard fits with that of Corinth rather than with that of Aegina whose coins Athens had used hitherto, and thus he helped to give a new direction to Attic trade.

(e) SOLON AND THE CONSTITUTION

Not all of Solon's constitutional reforms[96] are relevant to the question of tyranny, but his fundamental measure, the distribution of political power to four classes briefly discussed on p. 37, broke the aristocratic monopoly in a peaceful manner which contrasts sharply with the violent means used at Corinth and elsewhere, and throws much light on the issues of the time.

The basis of the classes was income in kind, the number of bushels of corn or measures of oil that a man's land produced. The richest class were the *pentakosiomedimnoi*, the men with 500 bushels a year, a name which relates directly to their income and must have been coined to describe the class. The other classes were defined in the same style, the men with 300 bushels, with 200, and with less than 200, but their names, *hippeis zeugitai thetes*, do not relate to these incomes and are probably taken over from a military classification: *hippeis* (horsemen) were the cavalry, *zeugitai* the hoplites, *thetes* (literally labourers) the rest of the population which was not much use in war. (The alternative is an agricultural interpretation, *hippeis* the men who own horses, *zeugitai* the men with a yoke of oxen, *thetes* the hired labourers. This has the advantage that the name *thetes* is directly related to the classification, but it is open to two serious objections, from the passive character of the word *zeugitai* in other contexts and from the fact that a class of *zeugitai* defined in this way should have a much wider range of income than Solon's class.) Solon's income-groups must correspond roughly to these earlier classes, or their names would not have been used, and this is some indication of the character of the persons who composed these classes.

By this scheme the nobles lost their exclusive right to office and power, but they lost only the monopoly. The wealthy commoners, the most conspicuous beneficiaries of Solon's reform, gained the right of admittance to high office on a level with the nobles. Though the reform was peaceful, its results were not secured without a struggle, which centred round the office of the chief magistrate, the *archon eponymos*. (It is disputed whether this was now open to the top two classes, or only to the highest.) In the fifteen years which follow Solon's archonship in 594, there were two years which appeared in the lists as *anarchiai*, that is, no archon was elected, or no election was recognized as valid, while in 582–580 the elected archon Damasias illegally retained his office for a year and two months after he should have laid it down. When he fell, a compromise divided the office equally between nobles and non-nobles. It is clear that the strife was between the old governing class, the aristocracy of birth, and the new men whose qualification depended on Solon's reform. After 580 we hear of no more *anarchiai*, and the reform may rank as established.

The *zeugitai*, roughly the hoplite class, gained access to minor political office. This was already much, for men who had had no rights before—the poorer members of the class may indeed have suffered as *hektemoroi*—but as we shall see, it was less than they expected. The *thetes* were given nothing but their vote in the assembly, but the value of this vote was increased by Solon's legal reform, which granted a right of appeal from the magistrate's courts to the assembly sitting in a judicial capacity.

Here we meet the principal difference between Solon's situation and the situation which confronted the Spartan reformers, namely that there was no difference of race or class in Attica comparable with that which divided the Spartan voters from the other inhabitants of Laconia. It is likely that the people met very seldom in pre-Solonian Athens, perhaps only in crises like Cylon's conspiracy (p. 84), and then only to confirm the action taken by the government, but when the people did meet, no free man was excluded. Solon, like the Spartan reformers, established regular meetings of the assembly, and from his time onwards legislation and major questions of public policy were always brought before it. For this purpose a probouleutic council was needed, but Solon did not use the old council of the Areopagus (perhaps because in 594 it consisted entirely of nobles and could not be trusted to give his reforms a fair run), and instituted a new lower council. Its composition is uncertain in detail, but it must be presumed that the *zeugitai* were eligible, and it is certain that the *thetes* were not.

The day of the *thetes* was to come later, as a result of the further reforms of Cleisthenes in 507. Their eventual dominance in the democracy was held by Aristotle to depend mainly on the rise of the Athenian fleet in which they were the rowers, and if Solon contributed at all to their power, it was by his institution of a right of appeal from the decisions of magistrates. Even here— so Aristotle insists, rebutting the fourth-century enthusiasts who traced all democratic institutions back to Solon—there was no intention to give political power to the people, and the fragments of the poems confirm that Solon believed in the control of the people by a governing class. By his reform the wealthiest of the commons had joined the nobles in the exercise of effective power, but a place was found also for the *zeugitai*, whose membership of the council secured them a hearing in the future.

(f) SOLON AND TYRANNY

In contrast to the early poems written before his archonship, which attack the greed of the rich and are primarily concerned with the problem of the *hektemoroi*, Solon's later poems are mostly written in justification of his reforms against the complaints of the *demos* which thought that he had not gone far enough. He rebukes their greed and complains that "those who gathered together for plunder, who had rich hopes and thought each one to find great wealth" had misjudged him: for all the mildness of his professions they had expected that he would prove tough in the event, but he had not wanted a tyranny, nor to share the land equally between the low-born and their betters. He harps on his own restraint, on the fact that there would have been civil war if he had given in to either party, and on the fact that he had held the *demos* back and not made himself tyrant. He complains, even boasts, that he had satisfied neither side, and reminds both of the benefits conferred on them. The *demos* had gained things that it had never seen even in dreams— but it would have been unsafe to give them more, for they have not the sense to cope with wealth. The rich and the powerful had been saved from indignity, that is, they had not suffered death, banishment and confiscation like the Bacchiadae of Corinth.

Solon's complaint and justification show us who it was that wanted him to be tyrant, and what they expected a tyrant to do. In outline, his job was to dispose violently of the nobles and to distribute their land to his supporters. Solon was able to resist this demand by dividing the opposition to the aristocracy. First he dealt separately with the genuine and substantial grievance of the *hektemoroi*. Then he admitted the wealthy to high office. That remedied their grievance and consoled them for any loss they may have suffered by his cancellation of the contracts of the *hektemoroi*. They did not want to overturn the system of government provided they had access to it themselves, and once they were admitted they had no further motive for joining with the revolutionaries. It was the class below them that would profit most by violence and confiscation. The leaders of this class, hoplites rather than *thetes*, formed the *demos* which Solon rebuked and claimed to have held in check. If they had been united with the wealthy commoners in hostility to the aristocracy, there would have been no alternative to revolution. As it was, there was no violence and no redistribution of land, nothing worse than squabbles within the remodelled governing class and grumbling from the *demos*, which had after all made substantial gains.

As for Solon himself, his poems impressed Aristotle as the work of an honest and fair-minded man who put the good of his city above personal ambition. Plutarch quotes some lines in which he pictures one of his shallower critics saying that he was a fool to reject his opportunity—"for once I had seized power, gained infinite wealth, been tyrant of Athens even for one day, I would have been ready to be flayed for a wineskin and my family to be wiped out". Solon's answer is that his milder action was a surer way to fame. An earlier, non-political poem begins with a prayer for the blessing of the gods, then immediately draws at some length the distinction between just wealth such as the gods give and the unjust wealth which men seek in greed: the one is a lasting blessing, the other involves a moral blindness which Zeus will certainly avenge on the man himself or his descendants. Solon, who was no puritan to deny pleasure, felt that the personal benefit to the tyrant was outweighed by the punishment which would follow soon or late. He is said to have remarked that tyranny was a fine position but difficult to step down from, and it is characteristic of him that he should regard the difficulty of resigning tyranny as an objection to taking it up.

From the public point of view, he preferred the stable and organized to the irregular and irresponsible. Not only was monarchy a form of slavery, the *demos* too presented a threat of anarchy : he believed that there should be a clearly defined and firmly founded governing class, and no unrestricted freedom. The wealthy and noble must have their rights, but even they must be restrained by law from exploiting the poor. His system embodies his preference for an ordered life, with its careful gradations giving each class its proper place, an intricate piece of machinery for the time at which it was created. On the whole it worked, for there was no revolution in this generation.

Athens has served as an example of the political effects of the economic advance of seventh-century Greece. The *hektemoroi* and the debt-problem were a by-product of the change from barter to a money economy, and Solon's constitutional reform represents a peaceful solution of the wider problems of the age. In different degrees, according to the pace and manner of their development, we must imagine these same problems affecting the other states of Greece.

CHAPTER VIII

ARISTOCRATIC DISORDER AT MYTILENE

THE troubles of Athens which were described in the last chapter are illuminated by the patient and resolute Solon, ready as politician or moralist to come to grips with the world as he found it, and not afraid to take the measures which were necessary to enable Athens to adapt herself to changing circumstances. In the same period there was a succession of tyrannies at Mytilene in Lesbos, ending with the ten years' rule of Pittacus which set the city on its feet again. This too is illuminated by a contemporary poet, but the light Alcaeus sheds is of a very different colour. Pittacus left no personal statement to compare with Solon's poems: instead we have the bitter comment of the aristocratic opposition, which upheld its inherited claims and resisted the change that was coming over the world[97].

(a) THE SERIES OF TYRANNIES

Mytilene had once been governed by the Penthilidae, who believed that their ancestor Penthilus was a son of Orestes and had founded the city as a refugee from the Heraclid conquest of the Peloponnese (p. 54: the linguistic and racial affinities of Lesbos are in fact rather with Boeotia and Thessaly). Their government collapsed at some unknown date, not later than the middle of the seventh century. The story was known to Aristotle, who used it as an instance of revolution caused by the violence of rulers and alludes to it in a tantalizing sentence of the *Politics*— the Penthilidae went around hitting people with clubs, till Megacles and his friends overthrew them: and later Smerdis killed Penthilus after being beaten and dragged out from beside his wife[98]. We hear no more of Megacles or Smerdis, but Penthilus might be the same as Penthilus whose daughter Pittacus later married. At the end of the century, when Alcaeus was young, the Penthilidae still retained the prestige of their descent from Orestes and Agamemnon, but other noble families had an assured place in the governing class.

The first tyrant in Alcaeus' series was Melanchrus, overthrown by a combination of Pittacus with the brothers of Alcaeus at a date which is given as 612/608 (that is, in the four years between the Olympic festivals held in 612 and 608): the poet himself is not mentioned and perhaps was too young to take part. But he was old enough to fight in the war with Athens which took place a little later for the possession of Sigeum near Troy, which in the end Periander of Corinth as arbitrator awarded to Athens (p. 50). Pittacus commanded the Mytileneans, and Alcaeus threw away his shield in flight and wrote a poem about it to his friend Melanippus[99].

The next tyrant Myrsilus bulks much larger in the poems. Several fragments refer to the danger that Myrsilus will make himself tyrant, and call on the citizens to resist before it is too late. Alcaeus' first exile was the result of an unsuccessful plot against Myrsilus, and took him only to Pyrrha, halfway across the island. An important poem written during this exile reproaches Pittacus with breaking the vows which he and the other companions had sworn, to kill the tyrants or die in the attempt. The combination which had overthrown Melanchrus was evidently renewed, at one stage, against Myrsilus, but Pittacus, by the time this poem was written, had changed sides and joined up with Myrsilus. The latter eventually died or was killed: Alcaeus called for the bottle, "now a man must get drunk, and drink violently, since Myrsilus is dead". After his first exile there must be an interval when Alcaeus was able to return to his city.

We do not hear the occasion of his second exile, but it was evidently part of a more wholesale expulsion in which the exiles had to leave the island altogether: Sappho too was among the victims. Alcaeus' brother Antimenidas went and took mercenary service with the king of Babylon. Later the exiles, led by Antimenidas and Alcaeus, tried to make their way home, and at some point they had financial support on a large scale from the Lydians of the mainland. They presented a serious threat to the city, and to meet the threat Pittacus was made dictator. For ten years he governed Mytilene successfully, then laid down his office and lived for ten years more as a private citizen. It is said that in the end he forgave and recalled Alcaeus.

(b) ALCAEUS

This is a tangled story. If we had more evidence, the various episodes would be clearer in detail, but the struggle for power between the factions would still be involved and turbulent. The best general comment, based on some authority who had studied Alcaeus, is given by the geographer Strabo[100]:

> "The city suffered several tyrannies at this period because of its internal divisions, and the poems of Alcaeus called the *Stasiotica* are about these: among the tyrants was Pittacus himself. Alcaeus abuses him and the rest equally, Myrsilus and Melanchrus and the Cleanactidae and certain others, and Alcaeus himself is not clear of the suspicion of revolutionary ambitions. But Pittacus used his power to put down the undue influence of the factions, and having put them down he gave the city back its freedom."

Everything that we have from Alcaeus confirms the essential correctness of this summing-up. We have seen already how he writes about Myrsilus. Since Pittacus' change of front and junction with Myrsilus, he too was the poet's mortal enemy, and Alcaeus attacks with zest his fatness, the squalor of his appearance and his flat feet, but most of all his low birth. Pittacus' father, Hyrrhas or Hyrrhadius, is said by the gossiping hellenistic historian Douris of Samos to have been a Thracian, and he very probably got this from Alcaeus, but in the Greek world, where Demosthenes' enemies called him a Scythian, assertions of this kind must not be taken too solemnly. The serious evidence for Pittacus' social position is the fact of his early alliance with the brothers of Alcaeus, and the fact that he was one of the "companions" (*hetairoi*) who swore an oath against Myrsilus. Anyone might follow a faction, but no one whose social standing was insecure would ever have been the "companion" of men like Alcaeus. The accusations of low birth are a consequence of the subsequent quarrel, and their value is in the light they shed on Alcaeus' mind, on his feeling that low birth is the most deadly accusation he can make against his enemy.

Alcaeus twice refers to the *demos*. The companions swore, among other things, to "rescue the people from their griefs", and in a later poem he complains that some god has "led the people to destruction" and exalted Pittacus. On each occasion he seems to mean the whole body of the Mytileneans rather than a party, and he shows no sign of thinking that the *demos* was a separate political factor which deserved consideration as such. Again, he may show some awareness of a general economic change when he quotes, as the saying of a Spartan, "money makes the man", or rails against "Poverty, the unbearable evil, which subdues a great people with her sister Helplessness", but his whole attitude shows that he took poverty as a personal evil to complain of and to combat, not as a general problem which called for state action.

Breeding is the unanswerable appeal. A poem connected with the struggle against Myrsilus contains the phrase "we must not shame . . . our noble fathers lying under earth". In the same spirit the Athenian lament for those who fell in the attempt to hold Leipsydrion against the tyrant Hippias in 513 (p. 101) describes the fallen as "good and noble men, who showed then what fathers they were born from", and the appeal to aristocratic courage and honour is the same through all the ages. The less amiable side of the same feeling is shown in a poem which attacked Pittacus' mother as well as his father: our surviving fragment ends with the question, "shall you, the son of such a mother, bear such glory as free men have who are born of noble fathers?" Only the noble can be tolerated in high places, which their fathers had held before them.

His attitude in the final struggle between the exiles and Pittacus comes out in a late poem written soon after Pittacus' marriage to a daughter of Penthilus, a descendant of the royal family of Mycenae through Orestes and Penthilus the founder.

"Now the man has married into the family of the Atreidae, let him rend the city as once he did with Myrsilus, till Ares is willing to turn us again to arms. May we forget our wrath again, let us have rest from the grief that gnaws our hearts

and the civil war which one of the Olympians has raised up,
leading the people to destruction and giving delightful glory
to Pittacus."

Alcaeus deplores civil war, but his only solution is to start it
up again and have the right side win this time—no uncommon
frame of mind, but one that left little hope of reconciliation and
justified the strong government of Pittacus, and his commission to
defend the city against Alcaeus and his like.

Such were the violent and largely empty-headed politics of
Alcaeus. The virtues he admired, courage and loyalty and open-
handedness, were real and valuable, but the conditions for exer-
cising them had altered. Alcaeus, idealizing the standards of an
earlier generation, wanted a unique class of nobles (cf. pp. 11–14)
displaying their virtue in the grand manner while the rest of the
community accepted and admired, and he could not adapt himself
to the real world of 600. The change in conditions soured the
temper of the aristocracy and exacerbated their inevitable feuds,
while the example of tyranny enlarged the ambition of individuals.
The seizure of sole power by one group provoked bitter resistance
from the rest : the result could only be chaos.

(c) PITTACUS

Pittacus is called king in the folk-song, "Grind, mill, grind,
for Pittacus grinds too, who reigns over great Mytilene". For
Alcaeus he was a tyrant, and tyrant seemed appropriate enough
for Strabo to use the word too in the summary quoted above
(p. 94): the folk-song meant nothing essentially different. For
Aristotle, on the other hand, he was a member of a special
class called *aisymnetai*, defined as "elective tyrants", some
appointed for life, some for a fixed term, some for a particular
purpose like Pittacus[101].

Aisymnetes is yet another foreign word, used for an umpire
in the games in the *Odyssey*, and to mean something like prince
in the *Iliad*, while the corresponding verb in Attic verse has the
meaning "to rule". It is the title of a magistrate in several East
Greek states, of various dialects—Ionic at Miletus and Teos,

Aeolic at Cyme, Doric in the Megarian colonies on the Bosporus
—and it looks like a word for ruler picked up from some tongue
spoken in Asia Minor. There seems to be no other trace of its
use for a special class of dictator, except in a doubtful story about
early Miletus : Solon would fit the definition, but we do not find
the word applied to him. Pittacus may perhaps have had the title
aisymnetes, but no other authority says he had, and there was no
normal magistrate with this name at Mytilene, as there was at
Miletus.

It would be clearer what Aristotle meant if we knew the other
figures whom he assigned to this class : as it is we must confine
ourselves to his definition and to the case of Pittacus. An elective
tyrant is still a tyrant, an absolute ruler who supersedes the
constitution, and to say that he was elected for a set term or a
special purpose tells us only that his rule was accepted in the
expectation that he would lay it down when the term was ended
or the purpose fulfilled. Pittacus might have clung to power and
transmitted it to his son, but in fact he resigned after ten years,
and this is the substantial difference between him and the ordinary
tyrant, and the justification for putting him in a special class.

In his early days, seen through the eyes of Alcaeus, he appears
merely as one among many competitors for power in an extremely
unsettled state. But we have not got Pittacus' side of the case,
and we do not know how he himself regarded such matters as his
temporary combination with Myrsilus. Apart from Alcaeus, we
have no personal tradition about him except what comes through
descriptions of the Seven Wise Men, a group which included
Pittacus as well as Periander and Solon. The writers about this
group were not much concerned with history, but used the figures
of the Seven to convey the moral ideas of their own later ages :
they transmit in the process a few facts which may be historical
(*e.g.* the length of Pittacus' rule), some sayings which may be
authentic, and some impressions of character. The anecdotes
about Pittacus centre mainly on his frugality[102].

The little we know of his legislation tends the same way, and
it was evidently intended to curb aristocratic ostentation and
irresponsibility. He limited the expense of funerals, which had
been occasions for lavish display, as we see from the funeral
scenes on Geometric pots. Here Pittacus is in line with a general

tendency of Greek society in the sixth and fifth centuries, but his imposition of double fines for offences committed when drunk was a provision peculiar to his own code. Alcaeus, who was not the man to approve laws against drinkers, retorted with counter-accusations of drunkenness against Pittacus' father and enlarged on the squalor of Pittacus' own person and habits. The political difference was also a difference of style and fashion.

Aristotle expressly says that Pittacus did not create a new constitution, only individual laws[103], so there was no wholesale political reform in the Solonian style. We may suppose that the Mytileneans had already made some modifications of their primitive constitution : for instance, when Megacles overthrew the Penthilidae (p. 92) the existing organs of government will have been altered, at least to the extent of admitting other noble families to the council. Alcaeus in exile complains of his rustic life, away from the assembly (agora) and council. It is probable, though the words of his complaint do not quite prove it, that he was himself a member of this council, and if so he was not the first of his family to reach this level, for Alcaeus boasts of his inherited position, not of one he had acquired for himself. In that case this form of council would go back at least to the previous generation, that is, at least to the middle of the seventh century. Alcaeus' words show that an assembly already played some part in affairs in his own day.

We need not expect to find at Mytilene a constitution so articulated as Solon's or capable of the same development. The government remained oligarchic till the late fifth century and allowed the demos no effective power, but there are many shades of oligarchy, and it would not contradict Aristotle's statement if Pittacus made minor and piecemeal changes for the benefit of his supporters and to weaken the position of the nobles. To understand him fully we need to know the means by which he was able to repress aristocratic faction, so completely that his resignation brought on no renewal of disorder, and to know in more detail the character of his supporters. We can be sure that his following included many whom Alcaeus thought unfit for public life, and from the little we know of his laws we might deduce an anti-aristocratic bias among his supporters as well as in his own temperament. But equally there may have been many in Alcaeus' own class who were tired of violence and prepared to accept Pittacus for the sake of peace.

Since there was no sweeping change in the constitution it is clear that Mytilene's trouble did not lie in her institutions. Peace was the main need, after years of strife, and apart from a few irreconcilable exiles, there was wide enough agreement that Pittacus could provide it. As Alcaeus put it, "they have set up the ill-born Pittacus as tyrant over the spiritless and heavy-fated city, greatly praising him one and all". Alcaeus provides the answer to his own complaint. The city, which had had time and experience enough to make up its mind, decided that it did not like him and his friends, but trusted Pittacus.

CHAPTER IX

PEISISTRATUS AND THE CONSOLIDATION OF ATTICA

AFTER the fall of Damasias in 580 we hear no more of the disputes over the archonship which resulted from Solon's reforms (p. 88). There was a further war with Megara, and Peisistratus as commander of the Athenian troops distinguished himself by capturing Nisaea the port of Megara, but there is silence about the internal politics of Athens till 560, the beginning of Peisistratus' career as tyrant. It was a chequered career. Like Pittacus, he seems at the start to be no more than one among several competitors for power, and there is a similar difficulty in determining the exact character of his party. But we know far more about Peisistratus in his period of power than we do about Pittacus, and we can form a clear picture of the policy by which he consolidated Attica as a national unit[104].

(a) EXILE AND TYRANNY OF THE PEISISTRATIDAE

There was a struggle in progress in the 560's between the party of the Plain led by Lycurgus and the party of the Coast under Megacles. Peisistratus, with the intention of making himself tyrant, organized a third party which Herodotus describes as *hyperakrioi*, the men beyond the hills. By the classic manœuvre of claiming that he had been set upon and wounded by his enemies —it still worked, as late as 405, for Dionysius of Syracuse— Peisistratus persuaded the assembly to grant him a bodyguard armed with clubs, and with their help he seized the Acropolis and installed himself as tyrant.

This first attempt collapsed, though Herodotus says that he conducted himself well, and before long he was driven out by a combination of the other two parties. As soon as he was gone they resumed their struggle with one another, and Megacles, who was getting the worse of it, brought Peisistratus back as tyrant. A tall girl named Phya was dressed up as Athena and it was proclaimed that the goddess herself was bringing Peisistratus back to the Acropolis—a device whose simplicity puzzled Herodotus by its inconsistency with the Athenians' later reputation for quick wit. Peisistratus married Megacles' daughter, but the alliance did not last, and after a rupture with Megacles he had to leave Attica altogether for a long time.

For over ten years he built up his resources. Eretria was his base, and it was no doubt with the help of the Eretrians, who had many colonies in the North, that he established himself first at Rhaikelos on the coast, and then in the silver-mining district of Thrace. This Thracian silver was one of his main sources of strength for the rest of his life, and in addition he raised contributions in money from Thebes and other friendly cities. Troops came from Argos (his second wife Timonassa was an Argive, whom he married not long after his first seizure of the tyranny), and he was helped also by Lygdamis the future tyrant of Naxos. About 545 he landed near Marathon, where his Athenian supporters flocked to meet him. The troops from the city made little resistance at the battle of Pallene, on the road to Athens, and Peisistratus was able to re-establish himself firmly with the help of his mercenaries and his money.

The rest of his life was peaceful and prosperous. He died old, in 527, and was succeeded by his eldest son Hippias, whose reign was equally peaceful till 514, when his brother Hipparchus was murdered by the conspirators Harmodius and Aristogeiton, afterwards honoured as tyrannicides. In the next year some exiles led by the Alcmeonidae seized Leipsydrion under Mount Parnes, but they were not supported by the people and the enterprise failed. Hippias, feeling insecure, sought fresh alliances abroad and began to rule more harshly at home. The Alcmeonidae obtained the help of Sparta, and though the first Spartan expedition to Athens was defeated, a larger army led by king Cleomenes in 510 expelled Hippias and brought the rule of the dynasty to an end.

(b) THE THREE PARTIES

Herodotus describes the three parties in terms which prove that he thought of them as geographical units, and Aristotle says that they took their names from the districts which they farmed. Aristotle also differentiates them politically: Lycurgus' party were the oligarchs, Megacles followed a middle course, Peisistratus was the people's man. Modern writers interpret them in social and economic terms as well, Lycurgus and the Plain representing the old landowning aristocracy, Megacles and the Coast being the party of commerce and the new rich; while Peisistratus has been taken as a mining magnate, as the leader of the city mob, and as the leader of the poorer farmers. There may be some truth in these political and economic explanations, but we can be sure that the parties start from a genuine local basis, since Herodotus and Aristotle agree on this point, and that the names are not mere nicknames like the *montagne* and *marais* of the French Revolution.

It is therefore important to determine the exact names and their literal meaning. Peisistratus' party has the name Diakrioi in Aristotle, presumably from his sources the local historians, and Diakria is well attested as the name of a district in north-east Attica, up against Mount Parnes and the Boeotian border, looking across the channel to Euboea. Herodotus' name *hyperakrioi* has a wider application: looking out from the Acropolis of Athens, the whole of eastern Attica is hidden by Mount Hymettus and is "beyond the hills". The precise meaning of Paralia, the Coast, varies with the context. In the legend of the division of Attica between the sons of king Pandion, a legend which is as old as Sophocles, Diakria is the north-east (as above) and Paralia the south-east. The land called Paralos in Thucydides is likewise the south-east corner, on both sides of C. Sunium. On the other hand, in Cleisthenes' redistribution of the tribes at the end of the sixth century, Paralia means the whole coast round from the Megarian border to the Boeotian, except for the immediate neighbourhood of the city[105]. Megacles' Coast need not be identical with either of these. The Plain is similarly ambiguous.

It might refer to the central plain in which the city lies, or to that and the eastern plain beyond Hymettus: the smaller western plain of Eleusis does not seem to play any part in the story.

The two names for Peisistratus' party cannot both be the original name, and Herodotus' *hyperakrioi* is likely to be the right one. He is our oldest witness, and if he is right there is no difficulty in explaining how the variant Diakrioi arose—it was a familiar name, Peisistratus' birthplace Brauron lies at the southern end of the Diakria, and Diakria and Paralia occur together in the Pandion legend—whereas if Diakrioi were the original it would be harder to explain why Herodotus gave a different description. Peisistratus' party, then, are the "men beyond the hills", and that determines the meaning of the other two names, which must belong to the area in sight from the city. Lycurgus' Plain must be the main plain immediately north of Athens, and Megacles' Coast is the stretch immediately south.

Any answer to the question what the parties were fighting about must take account of these locations. Herodotus merely states the fact that they fought, and it is left to Aristotle to give an explanation, a political account in terms of oligarchy and the *demos*. In the *Politics* this is assimilated to his general theory of tyranny (p. 18) and Peisistratus appears as the champion of the people against the rich men of the Plain[106]. In his *Constitution of Athens* he adds the Coast as a "middle party", and this agrees with the fact that Megacles was able to ally himself at different times with either of the other leaders, whereas no alliance took place between Lycurgus and Peisistratus. Lycurgus, then, was an extremist, and a natural interpretation of his party is that the Plain belonged to the older aristocracy, who still resented Solon's inroad on their monopoly. If so, the Coast should represent the new rich whom Solon had admitted to the archonship, and Peisistratus the *demos* which Solon had not fully satisfied. The old and new nobility might well be ready to combine against this *demos*, and equally the new rich might seek the help of the *demos* when the old aristocracy tried to withhold the benefits of Solon's reform.

But the geographical names do not wholly suit this interpretation. Plain may seem well enough for the old aristocracy and Coast for the new rich whose wealth was based on commerce, but already there is some doubt: the old aristocracy had local origins in all the districts which united to form Attica and their estates should not be concentrated in the central plain, while the new rich, when they bought land, had no reason to prefer land near the coast. In the case of Peisistratus the discrepancy is more glaring. The *demos* was not concentrated on one side of Hymettus, and eastern Attica contains both rich and poor land. If *hyperakrioi* is distinctive as a name, the line of division can hardly be economic or constitutional.

It must further be remembered that the reforms of Solon had eased the tension which elsewhere produced tyranny, and that Athens had had a full generation since 594 to assimilate this reform. Peisistratus' two failures to establish a tyranny and his eventual triumph organized from abroad do not look like the career of a social revolutionary leader. The most natural explanation of the local names is that the nucleus of each party was the local following of its leader. Plain and Coast were groups centred in the neighbourhood of Athens, already in existence before Peisistratus' activity began. The name of his new group, if it is to be a significant name, must mean that he claimed to lead a revolt of the outlying parts of Attica against the dominance of the city and against both its factions alike, and his nucleus was naturally beyond the hills, in the area of his home town Brauron.

No personal details are known about Lycurgus, but his later namesake the fourth-century politician belonged to the family Eteoboutadae, of the oldest nobility of Athens, and this may be the family of our Lycurgus too.

We are much better informed about Megacles' family the Alcmeonidae[107], which played a highly individual role in Athenian politics for two and a half centuries. His grandfather Megacles was archon when Cylon seized the Acropolis (p. 84), and because Cylon's supporters had sacrilegiously been dragged from the altars to their death the Alcmeonidae laboured under an inherited curse, remembered when current politics made it convenient to remember. The history of their various exiles is obscure, but the archon Megacles' son Alcmeon either held or regained his place in Athens and commanded the contingent which took part in the Sacred War in the 590's (p. 60). Herodotus tells how he visited the king of Lydia, was offered as much gold as he could carry out from the king's treasury, and staggered away with his boots and his hair and his clothes loaded with gold dust. To deduce from this that the family fortunes rested on trade with Lydia is to deduce more than the light-hearted story will stand, but there is no doubt of the fact of Alcmeon's wealth, and he won a chariot race at Olympia, which no man of ordinary fortune could afford.

His son, the Megacles now in question, had married Agariste daughter of Cleisthenes of Sicyon (p. 61), which both increased the family's prestige and did something to mark them off from the old style of aristocrat. In succeeding generations they took a more radical turn: Megacles' son Cleisthenes, named after his Sicyonian grandfather, was the main architect of the new Athenian democracy set up after the fall of the tyranny, and though the male line is less distinguished thereafter, both Pericles and Alcibiades were born of Alcmeonid mothers and consciously inherited the family tradition.

Peisistratus traced his descent from Nestor and could claim thereby connection with early kings of Attica, but his family has left no public record from before his time. He must have made his mark already before he was given command of the Athenian forces against Megara, and his capture of Nisaea strengthened his position. He had moreover the support of another powerful family from Brauron, the house of Miltiades[108].

This Miltiades, uncle and namesake of the victor of Marathon, eventually left Athens with a large following and was installed as "tyrant" in the Thracian Chersonese (the Gallipoli peninsula) at the invitation of a native tribe. Herodotus' description of this venture tells us that Peisistratus at this time held power at Athens, but that Miltiades had great influence too, since his house maintained four-horse chariots and traced its descent from Ajax; and that he left Athens because he disliked the rule of Peisistratus. It may be true that his departure suited both himself and Peisistratus, but he could not have taken his colonists from Athens without Peisistratus' goodwill, and Peisistratus would not want an enemy established beside the Hellespont. Miltiades' position is rather that of a supporter whose influence is too powerful for his leader's comfort.

Miltiades' family was connected by marriage with the Cypselidae of Corinth, and one member of it, Hippocleides, nearly won
the hand of Agariste of Sicyon (p. 61). Their race-horses prove
their wealth, and Miltiades himself won a victory at Olympia.
Hippocleides was archon in 566 when the Great Panathenaea
were established[109], a four-yearly festival of Athena which played
its part in Peisistratus' later policy, and the families were probably
working together already in Hippocleides' time. Miltiades'
expedition to the Chersonese is paralleled by Peisistratus' own
re-establishment of Athenian control at Sigeum near Troy (for
the earlier occupation see pp. 50, 93), which gave Athens a footing
on both sides of the straits. The close but uneasy relations
between the two families can be seen in the later transactions to be
described in the next section.

This important instance gives some idea of the way in which
Peisistratus' party was built up. The two older parties had
probably a similar local and personal structure: they may have
been divided by principle also, the one claiming and the other
resisting the benefit of Solon's reform, but this view of them
should be supported not so much by the names of the parties as
by the character of the Alcmeonidae and the actions of Megacles,
and the probability that Lycurgus belonged to the older nobility.

Peisistratus' third party was formed, Herodotus says, for
the purpose of making him tyrant. At first it was not strong
enough to maintain itself, but in the ten-year interval after his
second expulsion the opposition crumbled. It would be helpful
if we knew the process. Peisistratus' money, we may imagine,
was employed for other purposes besides the hiring of troops, and
propaganda will have played a part—Herodotus tells us of a
soothsayer who uttered an encouraging oracle before the battle
of Pallene, and after the battle Peisistratus sent his sons to ride
round among the fugitives and reassure them about their lives
and property: there will have been more to this effect, before the
landing. Most of all, one may suspect, the two other factions had
gone on bickering too long. Peisistratus had governed well,
Herodotus says, in his first short tyranny, and by the time of his
return Athens was ready for a spell of settled government.

We know from Solon's own words that he lived to a great
age, and some lines of his are quoted as referring to Peisistratus'

tyranny. The Athenians must not blame the gods, he said, "for you yourselves have made these men great by giving them support, and that is why you have fallen into evil slavery: each one of you walks with the steps of a fox, but taken all together your mind is vain. For you look to the tongue and the words of a crafty man, and you do not see the deed which is being done." This refers to some definite situation, apparently to Peisistratus' bodyguard and the first seizure of power, and also to the eloquence which other authorities credit him with. It shows what Solon thought of the political intrigues which made Peisistratus' rise possible. Another time he speaks more generally: snow and hail come from the cloud, thunder from lightning, "but a city's ruin comes from great men, and the people in their folly fall into the slavery of a monarch". Solon had tried to save Athens by constitutional means, but his laws could not by themselves repress the ambitious manœuvres of the faction leaders: for that, it seemed, it was necessary for the most efficient of those leaders to attain power above the constitution, and Solon saw that as the ruin of his work[110].

(c) THE MAINTENANCE OF POWER

Peisistratus had defeated the forces of the city in battle, and his mercenary army enabled him to suppress any further resistance. To overturn the government was one thing, to provide an alternative was another, for it is not true that

> the same Arts that did gain
> a Pow'r must it maintain.

Peisistratus' arts of government need a separate section.

He had the advantage that Solon's reform had dealt already with the problem of aristocratic privilege, and provided an up-to-date machinery for the daily government of the state. The problem must have been harder for Cypselus, who swept away government and governing class together and had to start afresh: Peisistratus could let existing laws and institutions stand, merely taking care that his own men were elected to office—as

Thucydides describes, stressing the importance of this aspect of the tyranny. He had an organized party behind him, and (though no ancient authority refers to this) the means of rewarding them, for some at least of his opponents had been exiled and their lands were at his disposal. But problems enough remained, including one which has often embarrassed successful revolutionaries, the problem of reconciling the opposition without offending one's own supporters.

Peisistratus' skill in conciliating all classes of the Athenian population impressed Aristotle, who devoted disproportionate space to the mere narrative of the tyranny in his *Constitution of Athens*, and a long passage of the *Politics* to the tactics of a tyrant who is only "half-wicked"[111]. The theme of this part of the *Politics* is the problem of conserving various kinds of government, and Aristotle distinguishes two methods of conserving tyranny. One, which he describes as "traditional", is the system of universal repression for which the models are Periander and the kings of Persia. Something has been said of this, as regards Periander, and of the weakness of a theory which has to say that the building programmes of the tyrants were designed merely to keep their subjects occupied and poor (p. 51): the examples of this include the enormous temple of Olympian Zeus begun by the Peisistratidae at Athens. Absolute rulers are of course bound to use repression, for strong government is never wholly popular, but fourth-century theory, with its opposition of the virtuous king and the wicked tyrant, had gone to such extremes that it could no longer give a plausible account of a tyrant as popular as Peisistratus evidently was.

Hence Aristotle's second method, which portrays a tyrant with the opposite object, that of recommending himself to his subjects by his apparent virtue. He must pretend to care for the common interest not his own, to be the steward and not the devourer of public revenue, to practise moral virtues and respect religion. The subjects must be encouraged to virtue, peace must be kept between rich and poor, or at the worst the stronger of these two parties must be the tyrant's friend. The "half-wicked" tyrant must look like a king to his subjects, and Aristotle adds the advice that he should deal with the upper classes by diplomacy and with the many by demagogic methods. The echo of this in

the *Constitution of Athens* shows that he was thinking of Peisistratus—"the bulk both of the nobles and the commons favoured
him: the former he bound to him by diplomacy and the latter
by the help he gave them in their private affairs, and he managed
both of them well".

This pragmatic, near-Machiavellian treatment of the tyrant's
position is in a quite different style from the conventional picture
of the suspicious and repressive Periander, and it fits uneasily
with other parts of Aristotle's theory, as his phrases betray
—notably the odd qualification that this milder sort of tyrant
must take care still to have some unwilling subjects, or he will
cease, by definition, to be a tyrant at all. But Aristotle was not so
bound by theory that he could not admit the historical tradition
that some tyrants had been mild rulers, for instance Cypselus
and the Orthagorids of Sicyon. For the portrait of the "half-
wicked" tyrant he must be drawing on the work of some historian
who gave a sympathetic account of Peisistratus and the methods
by which he gained and kept his popularity.

We cannot follow Peisistratus' dealings with the noble families
at all fully, but chance has recently given us a fragment from a
list of archons covering the years 528–521, which illustrates the
way in which the Athenian tyranny handled its problem—not a
representative sample, but a significant one, since these are the
opening years of Hippias' reign, when special care was needed to
smooth the succession. Peisistratus died in the year 528/7. The
next year 527/6 gives us the first name on the new list, Onetor or
Onetorides, not so far as we know a name of political significance:
perhaps Peisistratus died late in the year, when the next archon
was already designated, and the appointment was not disturbed.
Then for 526/5 we have Hippias himself, followed by Cleisthenes
(525/4), Miltiades (524/3), Calliades (523/2), and Hippias' son
the younger Peisistratus (522/1)[112].

Cleisthenes is the son of the Alcmeonid Megacles, Peisistratus'
old rival. Herodotus, hostile to the tyranny and ready to believe
well of his patron Pericles' family, will have it that the Alcmeonidae
were in exile from the start of the tyranny, but this document
shows that the exile was not so complete or so continuous, and
Cleisthenes was in Athens at Hippias' accession, the first to
receive, and accept, from him nomination to the chief magistracy.

We do not know how or when he quarrelled with Hippias, but by the end of the reign he was in exile and led the movement against the tyrants.

His successor in the archonship is the younger Miltiades, son of Cimon the half-brother of the elder Miltiades who went to the Chersonese[113]. Cimon was fully as wealthy as his half-brother, and since the latter was childless he was the head of the family in Athens and a formidable figure, though reputed to be stupid. He had the unusual distinction of winning the four-horse chariot race at Olympia three times running with the same team. The political value of his wealth needs no comment, and the importance attached to an Olympic victory will appear from the frequency with which such victories have been mentioned in this chapter alone. Greek feeling goes far beyond anything we might feel about a Derby winner, as any poem of Pindar shows, or the fact that victors in the greater games received free meals at the archon's table at Athens; a successful stable was a serious political asset.

Cimon quarrelled with Peisistratus, and was in exile when he won his first victory in 536. The second time, in 532, he had the victory proclaimed in Peisistratus' name not his own, and was reconciled to him and returned to Athens. The third was in 528, and not long after he was murdered, Herodotus says by the sons of Peisistratus, their father being no longer alive: it is intelligible that Cimon might be dangerous to the new tyrant before his position was secured. But if the Peisistratidae were guilty, they concealed the fact and befriended Miltiades: this archonship will be one of the favours which they did him (and he accepted), and later, when the succession in the Chersonese fell vacant, they sent him out there. Later still, he returned and led the Athenian troops to victory at Marathon in 490.

Calliades is not known to us in his own right, and since the names Calliades and Callias are common among the upper classes at Athens we cannot identify his family: but we may fairly judge his importance from the company in which we find him.

Thus for the first five archonships of the new reign we have first the tyrant himself, then the representatives of two or three leading families, and when their claims have been satisfied the tyrant's son was started on his career. This will serve as an illustration of the dealings of the Peisistratidae with the noble families. By these and other favours they were able to bring enough of them into the government to make it workable. It was of course among the upper classes, who regarded government as their right, that opposition to a tyranny was most to be feared, but for the time being the tyrant could at least offer a young man a career, and the alternative was mute opposition or exile.

As regards his benefits to the people, Aristotle singles out Peisistratus' encouragement of the small farmer. He levied a tax on agricultural produce (Thucydides says it was five per cent, and describes it as a moderate burden), but returned some of it to the land in the form of loans to struggling farmers. He is recorded to have made tours of personal inspection, and his institution of travelling judges to settle smaller disputes in the country saved the countryman the necessity of coming to Athens for small matters, helped to make justice more uniform, and strengthened the central government. In the middle of the fifth century, when Thucydides and Aristophanes were young, Attica was not only an industrial and commercial state, but a state of prosperous small farmers, and Peisistratus should have much of the credit for this.

The famous public works of the tyranny gave employment to many, as those of Pericles did later: the temple of Athena Parthenos on the Acropolis, destroyed by the Persians in 480 and eventually replaced by Pericles' Parthenon; the great temple begun for Olympian Zeus; and the fountain-house called Enneakrounos, the Nine Springs—Greece is a thirsty land, and many of the tyrants took care for their city's water supply. Besides these works directly set on foot by the tyrants, Attic industry prospered in general. Our best index is the pottery, whose quality we can still see and whose export we can trace in detail.

This is the time when the pottery industry of Athens grew to maturity and overwhelmed the products of all other cities. The black-figure style was reaching its height when Peisistratus seized power, and was exported all over the Greek trading area, as far as Etruria and Southern Russia: it gave way to the earliest red-figure at the beginning of Hippias' reign. The growth of a great school of Attic sculptors was slower, but the tyranny saw the earliest of the series of female statues

called the Korai and other developments in temple sculpture.
Apart from individual patronage, it is hard to estimate
exactly how much help was given by the tyrants to the pottery
and other industries. Neither now nor later was Attic industry
controlled or organized by the state, but much can be done
without direct control. Peisistratus, having an ampler supply of
silver than had been available before, improved the Attic coinage
and increased the amount of coin in circulation. The oil-jars
which were given in large numbers as prizes at the Panathenaea
were not only a regular order for the potters but an advertisement
for Attic oil. There will have been other measures with the same
tendency.

Indirectly the tyranny helped Attic prosperity by the internal
and external peace it provided. Enough has been said of internal
affairs already. Abroad, Peisistratus had wide connections before
his final establishment as tyrant (p. 101), and we hear at a later
stage that the dynasty was on the friendliest terms with Sparta
too. Peisistratus did not, like many autocrats, attempt to unite
the nation behind him by foreign aggression: there were no
mainland wars, Megara was quiet, and Athens was secure in
possession of Salamis.

Peisistratus' positive activity was in the Hellespont area and
the Aegean. One of his earliest acts was to help his ally Lygdamis
to the tyranny of Naxos, and later he purified Delos by opening
all graves in sight of the sanctuary and burying the bodies elsewhere—Delos was an Ionian sanctuary, and this is a slight
assertion of that primacy among the Ionians which Athens was
to exploit to the full in the next century. In the Hellespont he
re-established Athenian control at Sigeum and installed one of
his younger sons as governor: with Miltiades in the Chersonese,
Athens had now some control over the passage to the Black Sea
and to Southern Russia, a market for Athenian oil and an
important source of corn. In the North he held his position in the
Thracian mining area and was friendly with Macedon, whose
king offered Hippias a refuge after his expulsion.

Positively as well as negatively Peisistratus' foreign policy
furthered Athenian interests. For a full generation Athens
enjoyed peace and prosperity, and in the main was reconciled
to the loss of that political liberty which the upper classes at least

had exercised in the previous generation. For all the harshness which Hippias is said to have shown after his brother's murder in 514, the common people did not rise against him when the Alcmeonidae fortified Leipsydrion in 513, and it was the foreign army of Sparta which ejected him in 510.

(d) THE PLACE OF THE TYRANNY IN THE DEVELOPMENT OF ATHENS

Whatever pains the Peisistratidae took to conciliate the noble families, the tyranny had suppressed the free play of aristocratic faction, indeed this was one of its principal services to Athens. Many of Peisistratus' opponents had gone into exile, and others had had to give hostages, who were deposited with Lygdamis on Naxos. He could not disguise his position, though he might play at being an ordinary citizen—the story was told how he was cited before the Areopagus on a charge of murder, and attended the court, but significantly his accuser did not appear : he could not be treated as an equal while he maintained his own army and lived on the Acropolis, and the discrepancy bore most hardly on those who were by birth his equals. Thus in the nature of things the tyranny was bound to have some anti-aristocratic bias.

Attica, small by our standards, had a large area for a Greek state. The aristocracy lived their public lives in Athens, but had local roots and strong local influence, and both Peisistratus now and Cleisthenes later took measures to overcome local particularism. We see this clearly in Peisistratus' encouragement of national cults, especially of the cult of Athena through the Panathenaic festival and the temple on the Acropolis. The festivals of Dionysus also received his attention, and he introduced the competition of tragic choruses from which the art of the great fifth-century tragedians grew[114]. Dionysus was a god whose appeal was universal, not the special preserve of a noble family, and Athena was the patroness of the city and the whole people, not of any particular section.

The mystery cult of Eleusis, whose priesthood remained in the hands of two individual families, became nevertheless a national institution, and claimed from abroad as well offerings of first-fruits to the place where Demeter made the gift of corn to mankind. Peisistratus contributed to this development, and he and his sons seem also to have patronized Orphism, while Hippias was expert in oracles and had a large collection of them. The religious beliefs of the tyrants are a mixture, characteristic of an age of transition : naturally they are not all, or even mainly, policy, but so far as we can detect a definite tendency it is anti-aristocratic and national[115].

The buildings served a similar purpose, stimulating pride in the city : again, there is a parallel with Pericles and his aim to make Athens a worthy capital of empire. The development of Theseus as a national hero, with a set of labours to compare with those of the Dorian Heracles, belongs roughly to this time. The Great Panathenaea, though not Peisistratus' own creation (p. 106), were celebrated with increasing magnificence, and Peisistratus added to the festival the recitation of the works of Homer. His sons' court, and especially the patronage of Hipparchus, attracted poets and musicians from abroad, Anacreon and Simonides and Lasus of Hermione. Athens was growing rapidly, preparing for her great centuries to come.

Under this surface the ground was being prepared for the democracy which was set up three years after the expulsion of Hippias. The essential factor is the effect on the ordinary man of replacing aristocratic faction by a stable, continuous and paternal government. Previously the poor man could appeal only to an upper-class patron whose political fortunes were uncertain and whose energies were mainly concentrated on party rivalry. In the tyrant he had a master, but a master whose position was secure and whose decisions were enforceable, and one who favoured the small farmer and adopted measures beneficial to industry and trade. Aristotle's description of Peisistratus as the champion of the *demos*, if not an adequate account of the way he gained his power, can be justified with reference to his use of his power when it was established.

The patronage of the tyrants weakened the dependence of the *demos* on any lesser patron, and the strife of upper-class parties was a form of disturbance unfamiliar to most Athenians when it broke out afresh, after the fall of the tyranny, between Isagoras and Cleisthenes. Isagoras got the upper hand and was elected archon for 508/7. Cleisthenes retorted with proposals for constitutional reform—as Herodotus puts it, he took the *demos* into partnership—and Isagoras was defeated in his turn. The details of the Cleisthenic reform lie outside the scope of this book : the general effect was to give the *demos* a direct share in the management of affairs, beyond what it had ever had before. Cleisthenes' proposals gained for him the support of that large mass of the people who had been loyal to Hippias, or at least indifferent, when an aristocratic group seized Leipsydrion in 513[116].

The temporary result, Cleisthenes' victory over Isagoras, is unimportant compared with the long-term result. In the fifth century the leaders still come from the upper class, but they have no constitutional privilege. The *demos* needed their skill and experience, but it was conscious of being itself the ultimate arbiter of policy, free to dismiss its officers if the results they achieved did not seem satisfactory, and jealous of any encroachment on its own rights. The *demos* now becomes its own defender and the patron of its successive leaders. The corporate feeling which made this possible was in large part the creation of the Peisistratidae.

CHAPTER X

THE THREAT OF PERSIAN CONQUEST

THE Greek cities on the eastern side of the Aegean held no more than the fringes of Asia Minor. The interior they hardly penetrated, but it was of paramount importance both to the mainland cities and to the islands off the coast what sort of inland power controlled Lydia and Phrygia, and what attitude it adopted to the Greeks[117]. At the end of the eighth century Asia Minor was devastated by Cimmerians from Southern Russia, whose raids disturbed natives and Greeks alike for the next fifty years. The king whom Greece knew as Midas committed suicide and his kingdom of Phrygia collapsed. A palace revolution brought Gyges to the throne of Lydia (pp. 21–22), the founder of a new and vigorous dynasty which drove the Cimmerians back eastwards, and also sought to control the Greek cities. By the middle of the sixth century they were paying tribute to Croesus, the last of Gyges' line.

Lydia by this time was a familiar neighbour, long penetrated by Greek influence, and the Greeks remembered Croesus with affection as a pattern of very kindly virtue[118]. The Persians proved sterner conquerors. Cyrus, the founder of their empire, reached the Aegean a little before 540, and Croesus' alliance with Babylon, Egypt and Sparta failed to save Lydia, which was overrun in one short campaign : the Spartan army, involved in a war with Argos, never crossed to Asia at all. The Greek cities attempted to resist, but were captured one by one by Cyrus' general Harpagus.

The Persian conquest of the East Greeks was felt both as a calamity in itself and as a menace to the rest of the Greek world. The Persians remained aliens and their governors were the agents of a distant power, whose help the Greeks might sometimes seek for their own ends, without ever becoming generally reconciled to its presence in their world. Even a good ruler, like Darius I who appreciated the quality of the Greeks, could never become their friend as Croesus had been. But at the time of Croesus' fall the most urgent question was whether the Persians would halt at the shore of the Aegean, or extend their conquest into Europe.

Cyrus himself turned back to the East, where he was eventually killed. His son Cambyses conquered Egypt in 525 : with Phoenicia, Cyprus and Egypt in. Persian hands, there was no independent navy left in the eastern Mediterranean but what the Greek cities could assemble, and their danger had evidently increased. After the death of Cambyses there was confusion·in Persia till Darius I established himself as king, and consolidated the somewhat loose empire gained by his predecessors. About 513 he crossed into Europe and conquered Thrace up to the Danube : his incursion into Scythia beyond the river was unsuccessful but not disastrous and the Persians were now on the doorstep of Greece. In 499 the East Greeks revolted under the leadership of Miletus and held their own for a while, but the revolt ended with the recapture of Miletus in 494, and in 492 Mardonius reconquered Thrace. In 490 Darius' generals crossed the Aegean, and though Athens defeated them at Marathon, the islands remained in Persian hands. The climax was the invasion of Greece by land and sea in 480, led by Darius' son and successor Xerxes, which was decisively defeated by sea at Salamis, and by land in the following year at Plataea. In the next fifteen years the bulk of East Greece was liberated under Athenian leadership.

The tension caused by the threat of Persian conquest lasted some sixty years, and while it lasted it was the cause of tyrannies on both sides of the frontier. On the Greek side it could be argued that the Persian danger created a special need for strong and continuous government—it will be remembered that Pittacus, fifty years earlier, was given his special powers to cope with the threat presented by Mytilenean exiles who were supported by the Lydians (p. 93). The Persians on their side could not trust their newly conquered Greek subjects, and the most economical method of controlling them was to establish in each city a Greek tyrant who owed his position to Persian support and would be lost if that support failed.

(a) POLYCRATES OF SAMOS

The large and wealthy island of Samos lies very close to the mainland city of Miletus, her rival in wealth and power and

her traditional enemy in war. Samos was the ally of Corinth
and Chalcis in the Lelantine War (pp. 40, 44), but Miletus the
ally of Eretria came off the gainer, and the seventh century was an
era of expansion in which she founded numerous colonies round
the Black Sea and took the lead in the reopening of Greek trade
with Egypt. Samian colonization is less conspicuous, but it was a
Samian merchant who first discovered Tartessus in South-west
Spain and opened up a new market to Greek trade. The importance
of Samos is shown by her share in Naucratis, the Greek colony
founded towards the end of the century on the western branch
of the Nile, whose management was vested in nine East
Greek cities who shared a common sanctuary, and three greater
states who built separate temples, Miletus of Apollo, Samos
of Hera, and Aegina (the only member from old Greece) of
Zeus[119].

Miletus' power reached a peak under the tyranny of Thrasybulus the friend of Periander of Corinth (p. 50), who successfully
resisted the attacks of the Lydian Alyattes, the father of Croesus.
In the sixth century Miletus was weakened by two generations of
civil strife, so that she put up no resistance to Croesus and alone
of the Greek cities made terms with Cyrus[120]. The lead was now
taken, in the first half of the century, by the Phocaeans, who
explored the Adriatic, founded Marseilles, colonized Southern
Spain and exploited the Samian discovery of Tartessus, whose
king became their close friend and ally[121]. But Phocaea was broken
during the Persian conquest, and after 540 Samos was left without
a serious rival.

The conditions under which Polycrates seized power, about
535, are not fully ascertainable[122]. There seems to have been an
earlier tyranny, which was followed by the government of a
group called *Geomoroi*, the "landowners". Herodotus, who
lived in Samos in his youth and might have told us more had his
interest in politics been stronger, says only that Polycrates the
son of Aeaces seized the citadel with fifteen hoplites, and after
sharing power for a while with his two brothers, killed one of
them and exiled the other, named Syloson. A much later author
adds that after his seizure of the citadel he sent for, and obtained,
help from Lygdamis of Naxos (pp. 101, 112). These statements
do not tell us whether, or in what way, the régime of the *Geomoroi*

was unsatisfactory, nor do they explain the brilliant success of Polycrates' tyranny.

We learn a little more from the seated statue found at Samos, whose inscription records that it was dedicated by Aeaces son of Bryson, who during his period of office exacted (a tithe of) the plunder for Hera[123]. This Aeaces, who is almost certainly Polycrates' father, was evidently a man of wealth and standing. The difficulty of interpreting the inscription lies in the word for plunder, *syle*, which covers many forms of seizure, including booty in war and the plunder of a pirate. The word is used in the treaty of two remote and somewhat backward Locrian communities in the fifth century, defining certain circumstances in which they would not seize ships at sea[124] : their activities are not far removed from piracy, which was always hard to suppress in certain areas of the ancient world. It appears also as an element in the name of Syloson, Polycrates' brother. We hear of seizures by the Samians in the period before 535, for instance of presents which the Spartans sent to Croesus, and Amasis king of Egypt to the Spartans, but we do not know the full circumstances, nor the justification if there was one. Polycrates himself is described by Herodotus as an indiscriminate pirate, who said that his friends were more pleased when he returned their goods than if he had never seized them in the first place[125].

This is an epigram rather than a serious statement of policy. Samos was no backward pirate state but a developed commercial city where trade cannot have been merely insecure, and Polycrates' seizures are to be connected with the wars which he waged for most of his reign. Herodotus describes in summary the rapid growth of his power, his successful expeditions, his 100 warships and his 1000 archers, his subjection of many islands and several mainland cities : the only incident he picks out is the defeat of the Lesbians in a sea battle when they came with their full force to the assistance of Miletus, and the use of the Lesbian prisoners to dig a ditch round the wall of Samos. Thucydides, who only grudgingly admits the importance of any sea-power earlier than that of fifth-century Athens, recognizes the strength of Polycrates' navy and his subjection of several islands, and describes his dedication of Rheneia (a small island separated by a narrow channel from the still smaller Delos) to Apollo. Polycrates' campaigns naturally interfered with shipping, and his enemies naturally called him a pirate.

These descriptions of Polycrates' activity give us some idea of his policy. The position of Samos, close against the Persian mainland, was such that he could develop a strong naval power only as Persia's dependant or as the leader of resistance to Persia. He took the latter course, and the rapid growth of his island empire was due to the hope that he could give his neighbours protection. His dedication of Rheneia to the Delian Apollo was a symbol of the leading position he claimed. Among the islands he held was Rhodes—a late rhetorician's story implies that he made his son the younger Polycrates its governor[126]—which was important to him both for its own sake and for his communications with Amasis king of Egypt. Samos seems earlier to have acted as the enemy of the alliance between Croesus, Egypt and Sparta (p. 119: the allies, perhaps, were Miletus' friends), but now there is a very well-attested friendship between Polycrates and Amasis, who had even more to fear from Persian aggression. It may be presumed that all Persia's enemies became Polycrates' friends.

Samos, like the other great islands, had always held some territory on the opposite mainland, and it was here that she came directly into conflict with Miletus. Polycrates, as we see from the story of the fight with the Lesbians, continued the war with Miletus, now Persia's dependant, and his expansion on the mainland was still more open war than his maritime activity. We know nothing about it in detail.

The war, and the weakening of her commercial rivals, were highly profitable to Samos, and Polycrates was the most magnificent of tyrants—there was none to compare with him, Herodotus says, except the later tyrants of Syracuse (Chapter XI). His buildings are among Aristotle's examples of the public works of the tyrants, and Herodotus devotes an excursus to the three main wonders of Samos, all of which should be attributed to Polycrates—the tunnel made by Eupalinus of Megara under a mountain to bring water to the city (it was started simultaneously from both ends, and the tunnellers were within six yards of an exact join in the middle), the mole which provided Samos with an adequate harbour, and the great temple built for Hera by the Samian architect Rhoikos. It is worth adding that the bridge which was built later across the Bosporus for Darius' European expedition was made by a Samian, Mandrocles[127].

The poets Ibycus, a South Italian from Rhegium, and Anacreon, an Ionian from Teos, settled at Polycrates' court, whose atmosphere evoked poetry very different from that direct expression of emotion in the vernacular which we find in Sappho and Alcaeus fifty years earlier[128]. Ibycus inherited the elaborate tradition of the choral ode as it had been developed by Stesichorus in the West, and wrote on secular and amatory themes in an artificial style, lightened by his delight in birds and flowers. Anacreon was for later ages the typical poet of love and wine, and anecdote and imitation distorted their picture of him: the genuine fragments show him a poet of simpler diction than Ibycus, witty and a little detached from the passions which he describes with good-tempered grace. Hipparchus brought him to Athens, where he remained and is said to have admired the early lyrics of Aeschylus.

Anacreon's poems are said to have been full of the name of Polycrates, though none of the surviving fragments refers directly to him. But they give us an idea of the glitter of his court, where other arts flourished besides poetry and architecture. The most famous name was that of Theodorus who engraved the ring which Polycrates valued most of all his possessions, and tried to lose in the sea. Another Samian gem-cutter was Mnesarchus, father of the philosopher Pythagoras—but Pythagoras fled from the tyrant and set up his school in Italy.

The story of Polycrates' ring attracted Herodotus by its moral, that success can be too complete and too continuous for safety: Amasis, alarmed by Polycrates' uniform good luck, advised him to get rid for ever of the treasure whose loss would most grieve him, but the ring returned, found in the belly of a large fish presented to Polycrates, and Amasis renounced his dangerous friendship. The truth must be otherwise. Amasis could not afford to lose a naval ally, and even the moral does not work out, for disaster fell on Egypt sooner than on Samos. It was Polycrates who broke the alliance, when he sent a contingent to aid Cambyses in his invasion of Egypt in 525. For this service he selected the most dangerous of his political opponents, and hoped to be rid of them, but they broke away and returned to Samos, where they forced a landing but were defeated by Polycrates. From Samos they sailed to Greece and asked for Sparta's help to overthrow the tyrant[129].

(b) SPARTA AND PERSIA

When Croesus looked around for Greek allies against Cyrus, Sparta was already the leading military power of Greece, and her position was secured further by the defeat of Argos in the war which coincided with Croesus' collapse (p. 116). The Ionian cities appealed at once to Sparta, as their natural champion, to rescue them from Cyrus. But the Spartans were unwilling to risk their army. Before his fall Croesus had seemed to possess a secure base in Lydia, and his own and his allies' forces were intact: it was much more dangerous to meet Cyrus unaided with a purely Greek force whose communications were all by sea, and the Spartans cannot be blamed for refusing. However, they sent a herald to warn Cyrus that he must do no harm to any Greek city, as they would not permit it. This was an empty gesture, in the sense that Sparta could do nothing to stop him, but important in that it committed Sparta from the start to an anti-Persian policy and showed that she accepted the responsibilities of her position in Greece[130].

Since nothing could be done on the mainland of Asia Minor, it was all the more important that the passage across the Aegean should be barred by a strong naval power, and this was the importance of Polycrates' empire to the Spartans. In 525 he went over to Cambyses. We do not know what pressure he was under, whether he was doubtful of his hold on his subjects or merely calculated that Cambyses was too strong for Egypt and the Greeks, but whatever his motive the Spartans could not be indifferent to his action. With the help of Corinth and their other allies they fitted out a large expedition to overthrow Polycrates and put his opponents in power. Their forces besieged Samos for forty days, but failed to take it and returned home[131].

Not long afterwards a revolt broke out against Cambyses, and on his way home to Persia he died, perhaps by his own hand, early in 522. For many months the empire was in confusion, an opportunity for adventurers of many nations to play for their own hand, among them Oroites the Persian governor of Lydia, who murdered his neighbour the governor of Phrygia and refused obedience to Darius when he emerged as king. But Oroites' troops preferred Darius and were induced to murder the governor, who was replaced by a Persian whom Darius could trust.

Meanwhile Polycrates had met his death at the hands of Oroites. Herodotus says that this happened shortly before Cambyses' death, and describes how Oroites lured him across to the mainland with the hope of unlimited money, and treacherously murdered him : but he assigns no very clear motive to the murder, and it remains obscure what the two were plotting and how they fell out[132]. At Samos Polycrates' deputy Maeandrius planned at first to establish constitutional government, but finding that resignation was likely to endanger his own life, he held on to power. In the end Polycrates' brother Syloson obtained help from Darius and the island fell into Persian hands, about 517 : an attack on the Persian troops who escorted Syloson led to a massacre of the Samians, and the new tyrant took over little but the wreck of his brother's power[133].

Maeandrius appealed to Sparta, but his appeal was refused : the Spartans, even supposing they were more successful than in 525, could make no use of Samos now its power was gone. Their next move was to expel Lygdamis from Naxos, where he still held his tyranny. The most probable interpretation of this is that they hoped Naxos would take the place which Samos had held in the defences of Greece, but Polycrates' conduct had increased the distrust they felt for tyrants, and they preferred to see an oligarchy established in Naxos[134]. The oligarchy prospered, and when it was replaced by a wider government towards the end of the century, Naxos remained a formidable power with a large navy, controlling many of the surrounding islands. In 500 it was able to resist a Persian attack ; but that belongs to the story of the Ionic Revolt.

(c) MILETUS

The Persian system of controlling the Greek cities through tyrants of their own nomination was a simple one, and needs

no long explanation. We find these tyrants assembled to guard the
Danube bridge during Darius' incursion into Scythia, probably
in 513, and Herodotus tells us how Miltiades, who was a Persian
subject now that Darius had conquered the European shore of
the straits, proposed the acceptance of the Scythians' suggestion
that they should destroy the bridge and cut Darius off north of
the river. The story may have been invented later by Miltiades'
supporters, but whether it is true or false, the reply of Histiaeus
of Miletus puts the position correctly: that each of them held
his tyranny through Darius, and if Darius' power was destroyed
their rule would be at an end, for every city would prefer constitutional government to tyranny[135].

Histiaeus and his son-in-law Aristagoras were accomplished
opportunists, ready to improve their fortunes with Persian
help while it lasted, or to turn their hand against the Persians
if it seemed more profitable. Miletus had recovered from the
weakness it showed earlier in the sixth century, and was now
more prosperous than ever: the collapse of Samos will have
contributed to her recovery and to the tyrants' prosperity. Over
and above this, Histiaeus began to interest himself in the silver-
mining district of Thrace, where the Persian conquest had cut
off the Peisistratidae of Athens from their Thracian mines, and
he obtained from Darius the right to build a city at Myrcinus
in the territory of the Edonian Thracians, near the mouth of the
Strymon[136].

But it was dangerous for an alien subject to become too rich
and powerful, and before his Thracian plans had gone very far
Histiaeus was summoned to Susa, and then held in honourable
captivity at Darius' court. Early in 500[137] his deputy at Miletus,
Aristagoras, was approached by some exiled Naxians with the
request to help restore them. Aristagoras saw in this a means of
extending his power, and asked for Persian assistance, which was
granted after consultation between the local governor and
Darius. But the joint navy failed to surprise Naxos—Herodotus
says that Aristagoras quarrelled with the Persian commander,
who then warned the Naxians—and after a four-months' siege
the enterprise had to be abandoned. Aristagoras was now in an
awkward position, and at this point there arrived from Histiaeus
a slave whose sole message was that his head should be shaved:

and when this was done, instructions were found tattooed on the slave's skin, to revolt from Persia.

This is the story as Herodotus tells it, and it contains some unlikely features. It is hard to believe that the Persian commander really gave his plans away to the Naxians, and it is a good deal of a coincidence that the secret message should arrive just at the moment when Aristagoras found himself in difficulties with the Persian governor. Throughout his narrative of the revolt, Herodotus shows dislike of Aristagoras, contempt for the Ionians, and a conviction that the revolt was an ill-planned and costly mistake. Without going to the opposite extreme, we must rate the performance of the Ionians in their six-year revolt higher than Herodotus does, and must not underestimate the abilities of its leader or his difficulties.

Aristagoras acted quickly. Before the dispersal of the Ionian fleet which had taken part in the Naxos expedition, he seized the tyrants who commanded the city contingents, laid down the tyranny of Miletus himself, and proclaimed the revolt of Ionia, which quickly became general. He then sailed to Greece for help. King Cleomenes of Sparta refused his appeal—on a purely military calculation there was no better case for risking the Peloponnesian army on the mainland of Asia Minor in 499 than in 540—but Athens and Eretria sent twenty-five ships for the first campaign, though they were withdrawn later. The revolt began well and spread to the Hellespont, Caria and Cyprus, and the Ionians gained command of the sea. It was some while before the Persians could organize any effective counter-stroke, and when they did, Cyprus took their first attention.

But meanwhile Aristagoras' position in Miletus had deteriorated. His resignation had left him in an anomalous position : he could maintain his leadership while the revolt went well, but when its impulse slackened, even before it met serious reverses, it was natural that his authority should be questioned and the acts of his former tyranny be remembered. Herodotus describes a council of his partisans held to discuss their policy in case they were expelled. Hecataeus the writer (from whom Herodotus probably had his information) was for fortifying the nearby island of Leros and waiting for a more favourable turn of Milesian politics, but Aristagoras preferred the plan of sailing off to

Myrcinus and the Thracian mines. He went, in 497 or early in 496, and soon afterwards he and his men were killed by the Edonians.

Twenty years later the Athenians undertook the defence of Ionia from the sea, and maintained it for two generations. They had behind them the full momentum generated by the Greek victories at Salamis and Plataea, and with their disproportionate power they could impose a firm control on their Ionian allies. The Ionians of 499 had not these advantages. Nevertheless, their initial performance was impressive, especially at sea, and the venture had a good chance, if the cities could be kept together and their forces exploited to the full. But though Aristagoras must have full credit for the successful launching of the revolt, his personal standing was too weak for him to control it through the long period that the war was bound to last.

There is no reason to question Herodotus' belief that in 500 Aristagoras merely intended to increase his personal power in the Aegean with Persian help : indeed, the story of the expedition to Naxos is hardly intelligible unless this really was his plan. Equally, we may accept the statement that Histiaeus desired trouble in Ionia because it might help him to escape from Susa, as in fact it did. But the dramatic story of the secret message is a simplification, and the plan of revolt must have been under consideration for longer, as an alternative resource. Herodotus reports a remark of Artaphernes, Darius' brother and the governor of Lydia, that Histiaeus had sewn the shoe which Aristagoras put on, and Artaphernes will have meant more than the single message on the slave's head.

Darius let Histiaeus go, on his promise that he would bring the rebels to order, but by the time he reached the coast Aristagoras had gone and the revolt was beginning to fail. Miletus would not admit him, and without a firm base where his authority was accepted, not even Histiaeus' resourcefulness could do much. As the Persians closed in on the rebels, the danger of disunion and treachery increased, and the final sea battle of Lade, off Miletus, was lost because the commander Dionysius of Phocaea could not exert effective authority and because the contingents of Samos and Lesbos deserted during the battle. The Ionians had now lost the sea, and the fall of Miletus and the end of the revolt was only a matter of time. Histiaeus, who had got eight ships from Lesbos, had settled at Byzantium where the Black Sea shipping was under his control, had seized Chios and begun an expedition to Thasos off the coast of Thrace, returned to Ionian waters when he heard of the fall of Miletus and the subsequent northward advance of the Persian fleet. In the end he was taken alive, and Artaphernes, afraid that Darius might yet forgive him, had him crucified without waiting for the king's orders.

The rescue of Greece from the Persians was not to be achieved by discredited autocrats like these: even Polycrates, whose position at Samos looks on paper so much more powerful than that of Aristagoras, could not resist the temptation to go over. This central and most fully developed part of the Greek world had outgrown tyranny. From the Persian point of view, the unpopularity of their nominees outweighed their usefulness, and soon after the revolt the cities were granted democratic constitutions and had their taxation reassessed on a better basis. On the Greek side, unity of command in the final war was possible because of the great prestige of Sparta, whose military pre-eminence was beyond question and whose will to resist was never in doubt. There could be no suggestion here that dangerous times required the strong hand of a tyrant. Sparta, secure in herself (Chapter VI), had gained her sixth-century allies by a crusade against tyranny and in favour of constitutional government, and this alliance, known as the Peloponnesian League, provided a firmly organized nucleus for the army which defeated the Persians at Plataea.

CHAPTER XI

MILITARY MONARCHY IN SICILY

THE Greek colonies of the West[138] were also confined to a coastal fringe, but the native peoples behind the coast were relatively uncivilized, an occasional danger rather than the organized menace which Lydia and Persia presented in the East. The Italian colonies were strung along the south coast and some distance up the west, controlling little of the interior. Further north were the Etruscans, a formidable people in the early fifth century: Rome as yet was barely known. The western end of Sicily was held by a few Phoenician cities, most of the remaining coast by Greeks. The Sicels of the interior, unlike the Italian tribes, were thus enclosed and more completely permeable to Greek influence: the Greek cities were often on friendly trading terms with them, but were also tempted by their own strength to annex Sicel territory. The real and recurrent danger came from Carthage, none too far away and readily called in when her Phoenician kinsmen needed help, or when the Greeks fell out among themselves.

The comparative isolation of these western communities, in a land whose native civilization did little to stimulate them, gave their history a peculiar rhythm. For long they leaned heavily on the mother country, and might be called provincial in their art, backward in their political and social development, but in saying this one must not forget the vigour and the capacity for experiment which they displayed in the classical period. Their growing cities, from time to time reinforced with fresh colonists, were less firmly rooted than the older cities at home, and the tyrants could shift whole populations, found new settlements, reach out towards a larger political form than the single-city state, in a way which was impossible for even the greatest tyrants of old Greece. The tyrants of Sicily seem rather larger than life and her convulsions too savage for survival, but she recovered from each with astonishing elasticity.

There were tyrants in the West before the end of the sixth

century, but their general importance is not great. Hardly anything is known of Panaetius of Leontini, whom Aristotle classes
with Cypselus of Corinth as an early "demagogic" tyrant: he
seems to belong to the last years of the seventh century[139]. Phalaris
of Acragas, in the middle of the sixth century, is a more widely
known name, both for the brazen bull in which he is said to have
roasted his enemies and for the letters whose authenticity Bentley
disproved. Acragas was newly founded in his time and may have
needed a strong hand, but the legend of his cruelty has obscured
his real history, and all we can say for certain is that his evil
character and the brazen bull were accepted as facts in the early
fifth century, when Pindar contrasted him with the mild and
virtuous Croesus[140].

It is natural to suppose that the descendants of the early
colonial leaders formed an aristocracy, and this may be the
case with the *Gamoroi* (landowners: *cf.* the *Geomoroi* of Samos,
p. 118) of Syracuse, though we cannot be sure how far the hold
of such aristocracies was weakened by the tyrannies and other
disturbances which we dimly hear of. In the late sixth century
oligarchic government seems to have been general, whatever
the exact qualification for membership of the oligarchy. But
conditions were changing: the colonies were becoming very
prosperous and less dependent on the homeland, especially on
Corinth, than they had been, and the people could not be wholly
unaware of the political changes which had taken place in old
Greece. If distant example was not enough, there were new
colonists who might bring new ideas with them, for instance, the
refugees from the Ionic revolt who arrived soon after 494.

(a) THE TYRANTS OF GELA

Syracuse appears to lag behind the other cities in the latter
part of the sixth century, and the movement which led to the
establishment of the Deinomenid tyranny began in Gela on the
south coast, where Cleandrus became tyrant in 505. He was an
important and wealthy man, the son of an Olympic victor:
Aristotle says that he led the *demos* against the oligarchs[141], a wide
formula (pp. 18, 103ff.) whose precise bearing in this instance we

cannot determine, though impatience with oligarchy is likely enough at this date. After seven years' reign, from which no incident is recorded, he was murdered in 498 and the tyranny was taken up by his brother Hippocrates.

The record of Hippocrates is purely military. He subdued the Chalcidian cities of North-eastern Sicily, Naxos Zancle and Leontini, and entrusted them to subordinate tyrants, Scythes at Zancle and Aenesidamus at Leontini. He defeated the Syracusans in battle, and threatened their city, but Syracuse was notoriously strong and he had no fleet to cut off seaborne supplies, so he admitted the mediation of Corinth and Corcyra and took as the price of his withdrawal Camarina, the Syracusan outpost on the south coast towards the Geloan border. He also made war on the Sicels: he must have conquered or terrorized the interior before he could march across to the north-east, and he was attacking the Sicel town of Hybla when he met his death in 491.

An incident at Zancle in 493 reveals Hippocrates' methods. Zancle and Rhegium between them commanded the straits of Messina (cf. p. 79): separately their control was less effective, and it was necessarily a grievance to Rhegium that Zancle should be in the hands of Hippocrates. In 493, the year after the collapse of the Ionic Revolt, a party of Samians arrived in the West to take up an invitation from Zancle for colonists to settle Cale Acte on the north coast. Anaxilas, who had recently made himself tyrant of Rhegium, induced them instead to seize Zancle itself, while Scythes and the Zanclean army were away besieging a Sicel town. Scythes appealed to Hippocrates for help, but when Hippocrates arrived with his army, far from helping, he arrested Scythes and made an agreement with the Samians to share the spoils of the town. He carried off most of the Zancleans as slaves, but handed over 300 of their leaders to the Samians to execute: the Samians however spared them[142].

This was realism indeed. It is true that Hippocrates, without a fleet, would have had some difficulty in expelling the intruders from Zancle, and that his agent Scythes might be blamed for having left the city defenceless, but Hippocrates' ruthless acceptance of the situation is not endearing. His reign lasted two years more, which were spent on the Syracusan campaign and on his last Sicel campaign. At his death he left two young sons, but the citizens of Gela refused to accept their rule: they had had enough of war and tyranny. Shortly after Hippocrates' death Anaxilas of Rhegium expelled the Samians from Zancle, and resettled it with men of his own: it was at this point that its name was changed to Messana.

The Geloans had reckoned without the army and its loyalty to Hippocrates' principal officer, Gelon the son of Deinomenes. He too came from a prominent family, the holders of a hereditary priesthood and descended from one of the original colonists. He seems to have helped Hippocrates to his tyranny at the time of Cleandrus' murder, he fought with distinction in Hippocrates' campaigns, and he was given the command of the cavalry. On Hippocrates' death he intervened, nominally on behalf of the tyrant's heirs, but when he had defeated the citizen army he seized power for himself. From 491 to 485 he governed Gela quietly (for a possible exception *see* p. 132): the Geloans needed a rest.

(b) THE DEINOMENIDS AT SYRACUSE

In Syracuse the oligarchy of the *Gamoroi* was losing its hold. Hippocrates appears to have hoped for a rising inside the city after his defeat of the Syracusan army (p. 130): nothing happened then, but a few years later the *demos* rose, in conjunction with the native serfs called Killyrioi, and drove the *Gamoroi* out. This first Syracusan democracy was soon in difficulties—Aristotle speaks of its disorderliness as a cause of its downfall[143]—and when the *Gamoroi*, who had established themselves at Casmenae in the interior, appealed for help to Gelon in 485, he easily overpowered the democrats and gained control of the city.

Gelon at once made Syracuse the centre of his power, leaving Gela to be ruled by his brother Hieron. Camarina, which Hippocrates had taken over a few years earlier, was no longer needed as a Geloan outpost, so the city was destroyed and its inhabitants transferred to Syracuse. So, too, were more than half the inhabitants of Gela. The oligarchs of Sicilian Megara, a short way north of Syracuse, fought an unsuccessful war against Gelon: the surprising terms of their surrender were that the oligarchs became citizens of Syracuse, while the unoffending *demos* was sold into slavery outside Sicily. The same distinction was made between the inhabitants of the small town of Euboea.

Syracuse was already the largest and wealthiest city in the island before Gelon's arrival. This was part of its attraction to him, but the main point must have been his need to develop a navy, and the contrast between Syracuse harbour and the shelterless coast on which Gela stands. His ruthless measures enormously increased the population of Syracuse, its prosperity and his own power. By 480, according to Herodotus, Gelon claimed to possess 200 warships, 20,000 hoplites, and other arms in proportion: he now controlled nearly half of Greek Sicily, and in addition Theron the tyrant of Acragas was his firm ally, bound to him by marriage. Their remaining opponents, Anaxilas of Rhegium and his father-in-law Terillus of Himera, were no match for them. When Theron expelled Terillus from his city, he appealed for help to Hamilcar the Carthaginian, already his friend, and Anaxilas joined him, giving his own children as hostages. This was the occasion of the great invasion of 480, contemporary with the Persian invasion of Greece and in its way not much less formidable.

Hostility between the Greeks and Carthage had developed only gradually. With the foundation of Himera on the north coast in 649, and Selinus in the south in 628, the Greek settlers had reached the limits of the territory which they could occupy without encroaching on the Phoenician cities at the western end of the island: Selinus indeed was not entirely a Greek gain, for being militarily exposed but favourably placed for trade with Carthage she was apt to take the Carthaginian side. In 580 a certain Pentathlus from Rhodes attempted to found a Greek colony in the Phoenician area at Lilybaeum, but was driven out. Carthage had no hand in this, but a little later a Carthaginian general fought an obscure campaign in Sicily, the first of many clashes. In 510 a Spartan prince named Dorieus made another unsuccessful attempt to found a colony in Western Sicily, and Gelon claimed to have fought a war in revenge for his death: nothing is known of this war, which appears to belong to the period of his rule at Gela[144].

The invasion of Hamilcar was on a greater scale than any

previous intervention by Carthage. He transported his main force successfully to Sicily and encamped outside Himera, where Theron's forces were, but Gelon marched out from Syracuse and inflicted a resounding defeat on the Carthaginians, few of whom escaped. The war was ended by this one blow. Carthage sued for peace, paid a large indemnity, and in the event left Sicily alone for seventy years. Her ally Anaxilas submitted, and was allowed to keep his tyranny. Temples were built in commemoration at Syracuse and Himera, and rich dedications were made at Delphi and Olympia.

Gelon's popularity in Syracuse is reflected in the story that he came unarmed before the assembly and offered to resign his power, but was confirmed in it or even hailed as king. He died in 478, before the glow of his great victory had faded, and his reign was looked back on as a period of prosperity and happiness. His brother Hieron succeeded him at Syracuse, handing Gela over to a third brother Polyzalus, but Hieron was less favourably remembered.

Hieron's great achievement was his defeat of the Etruscans in 474 at Cumae, far to the north in the bay of Naples. The Cumaeans had suffered in the previous century from Etruscan expansion southwards into Campania, and the Etruscan alliance with Carthage menaced the outlying Greek settlements of the West. Hieron's victory checked this process, though some areas such as Corsica were already permanently lost to the Greeks, and though further campaigns against the Etruscans were needed later. We hear of other interventions in Italy, at Sybaris, Locri and Rhegium.

Gelon had left the Chalcidian cities of North-eastern Sicily in comparative peace, but Hieron subjected them to the familiar process of rearrangement and transplantation. The inhabitants of Naxos and Catane were moved to Leontini, and on the territory of Catane he founded a new city named Aetna, for colonists from Syracuse and the Peloponnese, to be ruled over by his young son Deinomenes under the guardianship of his kinsman Chromius. The foundation of Aetna was Hieron's great pride, celebrated by Pindar along with his victories in the games, and by Aeschylus in a play of unusual structure written for the occasion[145].

The wealth of the Deinomenid tyrants was very great by

Greek standards. It was displayed to the Greek world in their dedications at Delphi, where, we are told, the wealth of the Lydian kings first enriched the shrine, and Gelon and Hieron ranked next as benefactors. We can see some reflection of it in the splendid ten-drachma coins with which Gelon commemorated Himera, and in the poems which were written for Hieron's chariot victories. Above all the magnificent, almost overpoweringly elaborate Sicilian poems of Pindar reflect the surface of court life, tell us much about the personalities of Hieron and Theron, and show us what Syracuse could boast of in Hieron's time[146].

But in the nature of things Pindar can only hint obscurely at the troubles which certainly existed below the surface. Early in Hieron's reign a quarrel inside the family caused the disgrace of Polyzalus and nearly made a breach between Hieron and Theron. Hieron suffered painfully from the stone, and seems to have been of a more suspicious temper than Gelon: certainly he is represented as being less popular. Pindar, in a poem addressed to Agesias who was a citizen both of Syracuse and of Stymphalus in Arcadia, remarks that it is a good thing for a ship to have two anchors in a stormy night, which seems to imply that Agesias' Syracusan anchor might give way. The tyranny held in fact till Hieron's death in 467, but his successor Thrasybulus, the fourth son of Deinomenes, lasted only eleven months. A quarrel between the supporters of Thrasybulus and the supporters of Gelon's young son gave an opening for revolution, and the tyranny was overthrown[147].

It is clear that the tyrants of Syracuse were of a different character from those described in earlier chapters, and that we cannot use the Aristotelian formula and call them champions of the many or the poor. Cleandrus at Gela may represent the impatience of the people under a restrictive oligarchy: Telys, who ruled Sybaris at the time of its destruction by Croton in 510, seems to have championed the *demos*; and in other cities of Sicily and Southern Italy the tyranny may have had this character. If we are to assign a single cause for the appearance of so many western tyrants in one generation, the obvious cause is economic growth, leading to dissatisfaction with old-fashioned oligarchies. But it does not seem that all western tyrants exploited this situation in the same way.

The Deinomenids began at least as the bulwark of the old order against the *demos*. Already at Gela the cavalry whom Gelon commanded for Hippocrates will have belonged mainly to the upper classes. At Syracuse he supported the *Gamoroi* against the *demos*, and his unscrupulous treatment of Megara is an even stronger indication of his sympathies. Herodotus reports that he thought "the *demos* most unpleasant to live with", perhaps Gelon's own phrase. The alternative to this tyranny was democracy, the constitution which Gelon overthrew, and which was set up again when Thrasybulus fell. When Pindar prayed that the benefits of Hieron's leadership might turn the people to concord and quiet, there were probably sufficient signs already that they might not remain quiet.

Hippocrates and the Deinomenids were also military despots with magnificent ambitions of their own. Hippocrates' conquests are all we know of him—as regards his treatment of Gela itself, we can only judge his character from his dealings with Zancle and note that the Geloans wished the tyranny to end at his death —and though there is no direct evidence, it would be a reasonable guess that he maintained a mercenary army, like his successors. There is no doubt at all about their mercenaries. We get some glimpses of the foreigners in Gelon's and Hieron's service: Glaucus from Carystus in Euboea, a boxer of enormous strength who ruled Camarina and was killed in a revolt; Praxiteles from Mantinea, the inscription of whose dedication at Olympia survives; Phormis, another Arcadian who dedicated a sculptural group at Olympia; Agesias from Stymphalus for whom Pindar wrote a poem; and there will have been many others. These are the leaders, and we are told that Gelon enrolled the rank and file in very large numbers as citizens of Syracuse, where they were a source of trouble to the democracy later.

In the inscriptions which survive from their dedications the tyrants give themselves no title and do not specify their position. The golden tripods which were set up at Delphi after Himera were dedicated by Gelon and his brothers as individuals, and the Etruscan helmet which commemorated Cumae at Olympia was the gift of "Hieron son of Deinomenes and the Syracusans"[148]. The tyrant remained a separate power, in control of the state but not part of it. Virtually nothing is known of the way in which the government was run at Syracuse: an assembly is probable enough, even if the story of Gelon's unarmed appearance before it is untrue, and a council, and there must have been magistrates. But itwas the tyrant who made the decisions.

The *Gamoroi* had lost control before Gelon came, and the democracy, shaky as it proved in 485, could not have organized Sicilian resistance to Hamilcar in 480: the army which Gelon led out to Himera is the justification of his violent measures in the previous five years, and a proof of the latent power of Syracuse and Sicily. His victory made him a popular figure in his lifetime and thereafter, and perhaps reconciled the people to his rule. But the political atmosphere of the fifth century was full of hope for democracy, and in spite of rumours of invasion the Carthaginians did not return: the national danger could no longer be invoked to justify tyranny. The upper classes, as time went on, may have seen the tyranny more as an obstacle to themselves than as a safeguard against democracy, and it is intelligible, apart from any difference in their characters, that Hieron was less popular than Gelon had been. In 466 dissension among the tyrants' party gave Syracuse the opportunity to try a new system.

(c) DEMOCRACY AND THE RISE OF DIONYSIUS

The fall of Thrasybulus was the signal for a general movement against tyranny in the West, and the uprooted populations sorted themselves out as best they could. Catane and Camarina were restored, Messana was given over to a mixed body of mercenaries, and only Megara was left deserted. Legal disputes over the restoration of property stimulated, according to Aristotle, the nascent art of rhetoric.

Democracy was now the rule, but it was never quite at ease in Syracuse. Aspiring tyrants troubled the city's peace, and the democratic leaders were so suspicious of opposition that it was sometimes difficult to carry on government at all. Nevertheless Syracuse prospered, and her preponderance among the cities of Sicily gave Athens an excuse to intervene in the West as champion of the oppressed. The great Athenian expedition of 415[149] was a test which the Syracusan democratic system seemed not quite to meet, and in 414 Hermocrates, a capable general who was suspected of oligarchic leanings, carried a reform which strengthened the executive by concentrating it in three generals instead of fifteen : but after the defeat of the Athenians full democracy was restored by the radical leader Diocles, and Hermocrates was deposed and banished. In the crisis of the Carthaginian war which began in 410, Dionysius eventually seized the whole executive to himself[150].

The Carthaginian invasion of 409 was on a very large scale, and was led by Hannibal the grandson of Hamilcar. Selinus was taken while the Greek relieving force was still at the stage of preparation, and though an army led by Diocles attempted the relief of Himera, the project was abandoned and Diocles left some Syracusan dead on the battlefield. Hannibal broke into Himera while its evacuation was half completed, and having destroyed the city and slaughtered 3000 Greek captives at the scene of Hamilcar's death, he took his army home to Carthage.

The next act was the return of Hermocrates, who had been in command of a Syracusan squadron in the Aegean at the time of his deposition. He landed at Messana, was repulsed from Syracuse, and marched across the island to the ruins of Selinus, from which he raided the territory of the Phoenician cities. His next exploit was to collect the bones of the Syracusan dead outside Himera and send them home for burial : this led to the exile of Diocles, but still Hermocrates was not recalled. At last he forced his way into the city, but was defeated and killed in the market-place.

Hermocrates' activity in Western Sicily alarmed the Carthaginians, and they returned in force in 406 and laid siege to Acragas, one stage nearer Syracuse. Acragas was well fortified and well defended, and the Carthaginians were at one time in serious difficulties, but they captured a convoy intended for the defenders, and the tables were turned. In the middle of the winter Acragas was abandoned after an eight months' siege, and serious political trouble broke out in Syracuse over the conduct of the war.

Dionysius had followed Hermocrates into the city in his last fatal entry, but was left for dead in the market-place and so escaped the fate of those who were taken. Since then he had distinguished himself in battle, and he now came forward as a patriotic democrat to charge the generals with treachery. He had rich and influential backers—when the magistrates fined him for his violent and illegal proposals, Philistus (afterwards his historian) paid the fine and offered to pay all others he incurred—but the main line of his agitation was against the wealthy and he demanded the election of genuinely democratic generals, securing a place among them himself. He also secured the return of Hermocrates' exiled followers, in the name of national union.

The military problem was the defence of Gela, the next Greek city threatened, and there Dionysius carried on a similar agitation against the wealthy, whose confiscated property helped him to raise the army's pay. But he had not yet done with Syracuse, to which he returned with dramatic accusations of treachery against his colleagues. It was conveniently remembered that Gelon had been in sole command at Himera, and now Dionysius was made sole general with full executive powers. Another dramatic scene—it is said of him, as of Peisistratus (p. 100), that he staged a mock attack on his own life—secured him a personal bodyguard, and from this point on he was undisguisedly tyrant. He married Hermocrates' daughter, and he had his most prominent opponents executed, Daphnaeus who had been general at the time of the fall of Acragas, and Damarchus who some years earlier had been appointed to Hermocrates' place when he was deposed (p. 137).

The Carthaginians rested at Acragas during these developments, from which they no doubt hoped to profit. In the summer they moved forward against Gela, which was less easy to defend than Acragas, and after an attempt at relief Dionysius evacuated both Gela and Camarina. After all that Dionysius had said, this new disaster was bound to provoke a reaction against him, but the form the reaction took enabled him by prompt measures to subdue it. The cavalry, hurrying ahead, entered Syracuse, plundered Dionysius' house, and treated his wife so roughly that she died. Dionysius by a forced march reached the city at midnight, and burnt down one of the gates: the knights were caught unawares, and his mercenaries surrounded and slew those who rallied to resist him. The army as a whole stood by him—they had seen his attempt to relieve Gela and understood the military situation—and the people were evidently not prepared to support the wealthy knights against him. Fortunately for Syracuse, plague prevented the Carthaginian army from pursuing its advantage, and peace was made without further fighting. The southern cities were to remain unfortified, paying tribute to Carthage : Messana, Leontini and the Sicels were to be independent : but Dionysius was recognized as the ruler of Syracuse.

He was not likely to be content with this, and the next few years were spent in rebuilding the strength of Syracuse and improving his own position. Land was distributed to his partisans and to the people, including some liberated slaves. The fortifications of the city were enormously strengthened[151], and the island of Ortygia (the earliest nucleus of the city) became a fortress for his residence. He is credited with important advances in naval construction, and he developed the catapult. Meanwhile he had to face one serious hoplite revolt, which reduced him to negotiate for a safe-conduct to withdraw altogether : but with his enemies lulled into false security he was able to make a successful sally from his fortress, and soon after to defeat the opposition. Again it does not seem that the city can have been united against him. Next he got control over the Chalcidian cities of the north-east, and restored Syracuse's dominion among the Sicels.

By now he was ready to provoke war with Carthage. The war was popular, and the Greeks began it with a massacre of all the Carthaginians in their cities. Dionysius recovered Greek Sicily, and used his new engines to capture the Phoenician town of Motya. The Carthaginian answer was another large-scale expedition under Himilco, which drove Dionysius back to face a siege in Syracuse itself. The city's new walls held, plague once more attacked the enemy's army, and in the end Dionysius was able to attack Himilco's camp and to burn part of his fleet. Himilco slipped away with the Carthaginian part of his army, leaving the rest to their fate, and Greek fortunes were restored. The war did not end at once, but after a few years a peace was made and a frontier established which Greek pride could tolerate. From now on Dionysius was secure in Syracuse.

The force of his character is evident from the record, but only a sympathetic account could give us a proper understanding of him. Unfortunately the history written by his friend Philistus was superseded in antiquity by the later version of Timaeus, which was violently hostile and represented Dionysius as a cruel and treacherous tyrant whom the citizens unanimously hated. It is impossible to give a coherent account of his rise in these terms, or to explain how he himself held power for thirty-eight years and his weaker son Dionysius II for ten more.

Aristotle, for whom Dionysius was another example of the "demagogic" tyrant, says that he gained the trust of the masses by his attacks on Daphnaeus and the rich[152]. That is at least half true : he exploited class feeling against the rich, both to secure his first appointment as general and afterwards to consolidate his power when he had made his temporary peace with Carthage. With equal adroitness he used the war panic against his predecessors in the generalship and against his colleagues, and also to obtain the recall of the followers of the unpopular Hermocrates. But it was not class feeling of this simple kind that got him the backing of men like Philistus, or the rich and influential Hipparinus whose daughter he later married. It must be remembered too that he had followed Hermocrates himself, and thought it worth his while to get the Hermocrateans recalled, and married Hermocrates' daughter at the moment when he gained his bodyguard and his tyranny. The link that held his various supporters together must be Dionysius' own personality, and their belief in his capacity : that is, men who were perfectly able to see through the shady manœuvres by which he sought popularity, were nevertheless convinced that he could organize Syracuse effectively.

The situation of Syracuse in 405 was desperate, and nothing could be done, once he had failed to save Gela, but make peace on what terms could be got. In the next stage, while he still clung most uncertainly to power, he made Syracuse safe against attack, so that when Himilco raised the siege the recovery of Eastern Sicily followed of itself. This was no small achievement. He got a footing in Southern Italy, too, and during the 380's most of this area came under his control. He founded colonies in the Adriatic, and intervened in Illyria. Twice he renewed the struggle with Carthage, but made no permanent gains : ancient writers reproach him for his failure to drive the Phoenicians out of the island altogether, but no student of Rome's wars with Carthage will underrate the difficulty of that task.

(d) THE AFTERMATH OF DIONYSIUS' TYRANNY

There were remarkable men and episodes in the history of Sicily between Dionysius' death in 367 and the Roman conquest at the end of the third century[153]. The Corinthian Timoleon purged Sicily for a time of her tyrants, and defeated the Carthaginians in 341 more decisively than they had been defeated since Gelon's time; the later tyrant Agathocles, besieged like Dionysius in Syracuse, broke out by sea to conduct a four years' campaign in Africa in the Carthaginians' rear; Hieron II became the friend of Rome and left a legacy of good government which was long remembered. It would be unfair to these men to dismiss them as the mere aftermath of Dionysius, yet Dionysius' reign was a turning-point in Sicilian history at which we may fairly stop to consider her tyrannies as a whole.

It may be claimed that Dionysius, like Gelon, was necessary for the rescue of Syracuse, that is, that no democratically elected body could have carried through the fortification and rearmament of the city with such speed and decision in the years after the fall of Gela, just as the early democracy could not have organized the army with which Hamilcar was defeated in 480. The claim is not to the credit of the Syracusans. They were able to overthrow the Deinomenid tyrants, and the potential resources of their city, witnessed by its great prosperity in the fifth century, should have ensured their future, but in the sixty years which followed the expulsion of Thrasybulus they failed to give their democracy a stable foundation, and though they dominated the other states of Sicily they achieved no stable relation with them. Turbulent and rootless, their democracy was plagued by attempts at tyranny, shaken by the Athenian expedition of 415, and overthrown in the pressure of the Carthaginian invasion of 406–5 which they could not meet.

The tyranny of Dionysius was allowed to outlast the crisis which had called it into being, and the price of the Syracusans' surrender to him was the suppression of political life as the Greeks understood it. After fifty years of tyranny they had forgotten how to manage their affairs for themselves, and when the city was liberated in 357 by Dion, Hipparinus' son and Plato's pupil, a member of the ruling house who had quarrelled with Dionysius II, the citizens could not come to terms with themselves or with their liberator. Dion, whatever his original intentions, became a virtual tyrant, and after his murder one petty tyrant succeeded another, the country was laid waste and its prosperity decayed, and the Carthaginians gained ground, till Timoleon came.

The freedom which Timoleon brought was freedom in the old city-state style, and Sicily in the middle of the fourth century had no longer the vitality to make use of it. The example of Dionysius pointed another way : if he had had a successor of his own calibre, a new sort of state might have emerged, stretching beyond Sicily into Italy and up the Adriatic, with Syracuse as its capital and the tyrant to hold it together. But the Greeks were not easily reconciled to this form of monarchic territorial state, and in the end Rome drove out the Carthaginians and absorbed Sicily.

CHAPTER XII

EPILOGUE

IN THE home land of Greece the Spartans had put down tyranny where they could in the latter part of the sixth century, and no tyrant could be tolerated inside the Peloponnesian League, where pro-Spartan oligarchy was the rule. In the naval empire which Athens built up after the Persian Wars democracy was normal, and we hear of tyrants in the cities of East Greece only when one of them fell away temporarily to Persia. But the Peloponnesian War of 431–404 destroyed the fifth-century balance of Greece. Sparta, with Persian help in the final stages, broke the power of Athens, and the widening of her sphere of influence altered Sparta's traditional role in politics.

In Thessaly, an agricultural land still loosely governed by aristocratic families at feud with one another, city life and city politics had not developed in the normal Greek way, except perhaps at Pherae whose port Pagasae carried most of Thessaly's external trade, and there only slowly: at the end of the fifth century a tyrant Lycophron appeared there, and was supported by Sparta in the hope of increasing her influence in the North. His successor Jason of Pherae got control of all Thessaly and was developing a formidable power when he was murdered in 370[154]. The Spartans were also friendly with Dionysius, and Spartan officers twice helped him at difficult moments in his early career, a point which Sparta's opponents made the most of. But it is not till after Sparta's defeat by Thebes at Leuctra in 371 that we begin to find tyrants in Southern Greece itself.

Not long after Leuctra, when the Theban Epaminondas invaded the Peloponnese, Sicyon went over to his side. A prominent citizen named Euphron[155], who had previously been known as a friend of Sparta, soon afterwards approached the Argives and Arcadians and represented that Sicyon would never be a safe ally against Sparta unless the oligarchy were replaced by a democratic régime. With their help he drove out the oligarchs and made himself tyrant. A year or two later the Arcadians broke into the city and recalled his opponents, and he fled to the harbour town below which he surrendered to the Spartans, though they soon lost it. Next, with the help of mercenaries from Athens (now allied with Sparta against Thebes), he seized the city again except for the citadel which was held by a Theban commander. In the end Euphron went to Thebes to make terms, and was murdered there by Sicyonian exiles, actually during a session of the Theban council.

Xenophon, who relates these events, was largely pro-Spartan and wholly anti-Theban. He puts into the mouth of one of the murderers a passionate speech against Euphron's tyranny and treachery, and records the murderers' acquittal, but he also records how the Sicyonians gave Euphron a public funeral and honoured him as the second founder of the city. "Thus for most men, as it seems, virtue is defined by the benefits they themselves receive" : that is Xenophon's sour comment, but Euphron's own citizens must be allowed their point of view. In the political disintegration of those times no small city could be secure among contending powers of far greater military strength, and the *demos* of Sicyon was less interested in Euphron's changes of side than in the fact that the oligarchy which Sparta had so long upheld was overthrown by Euphron's means.

In the following decades the disintegration of Greece went further. Athens had re-created a shadow of her naval league in the 370's, but it broke down[156], and in the 350's no Greek power could protect or very much influence the islands of the eastern Aegean, which were subject to new pressures from the Asiatic mainland, especially from the ambitious Mausolus who was both a hereditary Carian prince and a Persian satrap. There was a crop of tyrants in these islands, and another in Euboea where Athens struggled with Philip of Macedon for control of the island. The final victory of Philip in 338 imposed a sort of political standstill, and he and his son Alexander were mainly concerned to prevent war or revolution within Greece while they turned their attention to Persia. In the following reigns the influence of Macedon was usually exerted on behalf of the propertied classes, while the democrats looked elsewhere for support.

From 317 to 307 Athens[157] was under the control of the Macedonian Cassander, who maintained a garrison in the Peiraeus

and appointed Demetrius of Phaleron to govern the city. Demetrius was a conservative politician with a pro-Macedonian record,
an admirer of Aristotle and a friend of Aristotle's successor
Theophrastus, and his paternal government was conceived to
some extent on Aristotelian principles. The constitution was
oligarchic, but not intemperately narrow, and only those whose
property was less than 1000 drachmae were deprived of the vote.
But the assembly of these citizens had little practical power and
passed few decrees. A board of seven *nomophylakes* (guardians
of the laws: they were instituted in the confusion of the 320's,
before Demetrius' appointment) presided over council and
assembly and controlled their proceedings, and in the background
there was the foreign garrison in the Peiraeus.

The rich were relieved of the heaviest of the burdens they
had borne under the democracy, the upkeep of the fleet and the
provision of choruses for the festivals, for Athens had now no
foreign policy and virtually no fleet, and the public revenue was
large enough to provide for the festivals: Athens prospered under
Demetrius. He also revised the Athenian law code. We hear most
about his sumptuary legislation, for his private life contrasted
with his public regulations, and hostile writers made the most of
the contrast: it was an elaborate system laying down in detail
the expense permitted for funerals and the number of guests
allowed at dinner-parties, and new officials were appointed to
supervise the working of these laws.

As has been said, Athens prospered under Demetrius of
Phaleron, but such a régime could hardly be popular. Ptolemy
from Egypt and Antigonus from Syria courted the Greek cities
by offering freedom, and in 307 Antigonus' son Demetrius
Poliorcetes surprised the Peiraeus, liberated Athens and restored
democracy. But no settlement lasted long in those troubled times.
The Athenian democrats were discredited by their slavish dependence on their new patron Demetrius, whose cause seemed
lost after his father's defeat and death in 301: Cassander threatened from Macedon, and so the democrats were replaced by
another group of politicians headed by Lachares.

But a fresh turn, after Cassander's death, brought Demetrius
Poliorcetes back in 296, and Athens had to endure one of the
worst of her sieges. Lachares was loyally supported, but Athens

could not hold out for ever and Demetrius re-entered the city in 294. Lachares was a patriot or a tyrant, and his melting down of gold from the temples was military necessity or sacrilege, according to the view adopted about Athens' policy: but in fact the time was nearly past when Athens could still pretend to a political will of her own.

There was more independent life in the two great federal systems of the third century, the Achaean League and the Aetolian League, and tyranny in the Peloponnese became an issue between the Achaean League under Aratus of Sicyon and the Macedonian kings Antigonus Gonatas and Demetrius II[158]. Antigonus did not interfere directly within the Peloponnese while he held the key citadel of Corinth, but he supported certain tyrants, of whom the most important were Aristodamus (called "the good") at Megalopolis in Arcadia and the family of Aristomachus in Argos.

Aratus and the Achaean League, in opposition to the Macedonians, set themselves to clear the Peloponnese of tyrants, and they succeeded, though in a somewhat strange manner. Aristodamus had been murdered in 251, but another able tyrant, Lydiadas, established himself at Megalopolis in 244. Aratus attacked the Argive tyrants persistently, attempting in turn assassination, surprise attack and open battle, but the Argives showed no enthusiasm for liberation: in 235 however Lydiadas, alarmed by Aratus' campaign and unable to expect much help from Macedon, surrendered his tyranny and brought his city into the Achaean League, in which he at once became a powerful figure. In 229 Aristomachus II of Argos did the same. The lesser tyrants were quickly disposed of, the Peloponnese was cleared, and the League had achieved a startling expansion. But the ease with which two powerful tyrants had become respectable figures capable of taking their turn as generals of the League shows that these are not tyrants in the older sense, but simply men whom their cities trusted as leaders whatever alliances or constitutional forms the times required.

A more fateful change soon drove the League itself to alter its policy towards Macedon. Cleomenes III, one of the last kings of Sparta but not the least forceful, had already done something to restore the military prestige of his city, and in 226 he carried through a violent reform by which he claimed to restore also the old system of Lycurgus. This involved redistribution of land as well as reorganization of the army, and the one was almost as alarming as the other to the well-to-do Achaean leaders, who were easily frightened by the idea of social revolution. Reversing the policy of years, they called in the king of Macedon, and Cleomenes was defeated at Sellasia in 222. That was not quite the end of Spartan history, but it showed conclusively that even the most obstinately independent of the old Greek states could not, in a changed world, build up its power to the level of the new kingdoms.

There is no need to follow out the process by which Greece fell at last into the power of Rome and finally lost all show of independence. The illustrations given in the last few pages show the part which tyrants played in the last phases. Some were agents of the external power of Macedon, some headed their cities in a last desperate bid for freedom, the most were simply men of ability who in more normal times would have held normal office and played their part in the politics of their city : it was the instability of the times that made them tyrants.

The early tyrants were also a product of the instability of their times, in their case of the breakdown of archaic aristocratic government. The reasons for that breakdown and the manner in which a new class took control have been discussed at some length in the main body of this book. The basic cause was a change in the conditions, above all the economic conditions, of Greek life, and the symptom of trouble was the incompetence or mere anarchy of the aristocrats. When the trouble came to a head, the immediate need of the city concerned was for strong government to repair the damage and pull the state together, and the tyrant's unfettered executive power answered this need.

But though the aristocrats of that time might complain that the traditional framework of their lives had been disrupted, the executive breakdown was not permanent. This was a period of hopeful transition, when the Greek people had the energy to create new political forms for their new needs, and the age of the atyrnts ended with the establishment of the typical constitutions of the city-state. Oligarchy and democracy, which seemed so radically different, were alike in this, that they had solved for their own times the problem of creating an executive which was tolerably efficient, yet under the control of the citizens. The great cities of the classical period had no need for the strong hand of a tyrant, and they were confident that tyranny was an evil.

The problem of the classical period was a problem of relations between states—the need to combine against Persia, the ambitions of the leading powers, the jealousies of the rest, and the obstinate passion of each separate city for independence not only in its own local government but also in its foreign policy and commitments. It is conceivable that a league under the guidance of a single powerful city might have developed in such a way as to give Greece internal stability and the power to resist external aggression, without destroying entirely what was valuable in the city-state system itself. One cannot be sure: in fact, the latter part of the fifth century was consumed by the rivalry and conflict of two leagues and two leading cities which destroyed each other in the Peloponnesian War.

This disastrous war was exacerbated by the ideological clash between the oligarchs whom Sparta supported and the democrats who relied on Athens, and it was prolonged by the practical difficulty of reaching any decision while one side commanded the land and the other the sea. Even when a large part of the Athenian navy had been destroyed at Syracuse, Sparta still needed time and Persian help to build the fleet with which she eventually won her victory, and after the war no Greek city could hope to concentrate in her own hands so much power as Athens had held in the middle of the fifth century. The prestige of victory encouraged the illusion that Sparta could order Greece to her liking, but it was an illusion: the Greeks would not accept her haphazard and sometimes brutal attempts to impose her control, and she could neither unite Greece against the Persians nor rule Greece with Persian help. Thebes, though she became strong enough to defeat the Spartan army in battle, was even less capable of creating a satisfactory relationship between rival cities, and Greece dissolved in a series of minor wars which opened the way to her conqueror Philip.

The constitutions of the greater cities show some signs of

strain in face of the problems of the classical period. The Syracusan democracy, never very firmly rooted, collapsed entirely
and resigned to Dionysius the task of organizing defence against
Carthage. At Sparta the regent Pausanias, who commanded the
Greek forces against the Persians at Plataea in 479 and hoped
thereafter to retain the hegemony for his city, lost the confidence
of the home government and finished by plotting to subvert the
constitution and seize sole power: Lysander, who organized
Sparta's victory in the Peloponnesian War and founded Sparta's
brief fourth-century empire, was suspected of similar designs;
in both cases the established government prevailed, but though
this is a proof of the vitality of the Spartan system in relation to
the city itself, it is still arguable that Sparta's constitutional
machinery was inadequate to the task of leading the whole of
Greece.

The democracy of Athens was confident in prosperity and
resilient in disaster, and did not lose its hold on the subject
allies till late in the war with Sparta. The ascendancy of Pericles
in his later years was sometimes compared to a tyranny, and
Thucydides gives some countenance to the theory that democracy
failed when there was no longer a Pericles to guide it, but still
Pericles was no dictator but a removable magistrate, who was in
fact deposed when the people turned for a short time against him
in 430, not long before his death. There was a moment late in the
war, in 407, when many Athenians hoped and many feared that
Alcibiades might seize power and take the direction of the war
into his own hands, but he did not make the attempt and it is not
easy to imagine it succeeding for very long. Though many of the
upper classes were suspicious and doubtful, the people held to
democracy, which survived the Peloponnesian War and was
extinguished only by the Macedonian conquest.

Thus so far as concerned the internal government of their
cities the strongest of the old Greek states remained satisfied
with the political systems which they had evolved, in their main
lines, by the beginning of the fifth century. The problem of inter-
state relations, the problem of "empire" which tormented
Thucydides, was not resolved: the restless desire of the cities for
full freedom could always be turned against the pretensions of a
single leading city to rule the rest, and no acceptable form of

combination was found till, perhaps, in the days of the Achaean League when it was too late to defend Greek freedom.

The inter-state problem itself was, or involved, an executive problem. One aspect of Sparta's failure after the Peloponnesian War was the absence of satisfactory machinery to control the large area which she dominated now that she had broken the power of Athens. The mechanism of the fifth-century Athenian empire worked more effectively, but if that empire had grown much larger there must have been an executive problem for Athens too. But the empire of Athens was broken, and the Spartan empire which followed it collapsed more quickly. In the ensuing chaos the great cities held on longest to their accustomed forms of government, but the weaker states were unequal to the strain of their situation and tyrants reappeared in the central area of the Greek world.

The cities of seventh-century Greece, in the process of evolving a new form of internal government, suffered temporary dislocations which were at once the opportunity for tyrants and the justification of their seizure of power. At the other end of Greek history, in the fourth and following centuries, a progressive breakdown provided similar opportunities and caused a similar need for tyranny. In between lies the great age of Greek political history, when the institutions which Greece had created were in full working order and there was no gap for a tyrant to fill.

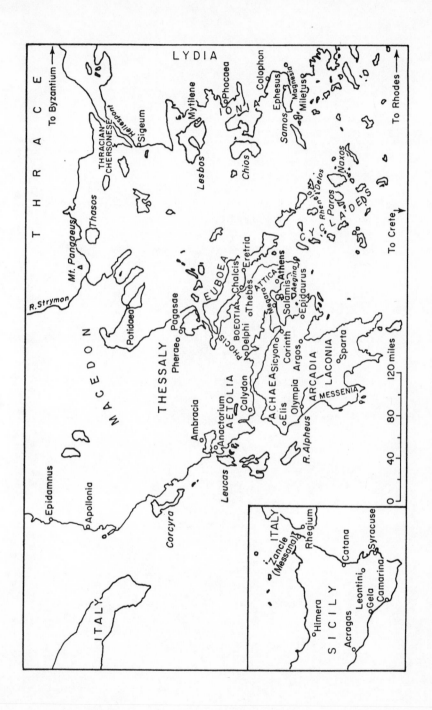

BIBLIOGRAPHY AND NOTES

These are intended mainly for the general reader who may wish to pursue further some of the topics raised here. For the sake of students of Greek history I have added some references (marked *) to ancient texts not readily available in translation and to specialist articles in classical periodicals: these references are necessarily incomplete but may occasionally save time. Archaeological works in foreign languages are cited for their illustrations.

BIBLIOGRAPHY

ANCIENT AUTHORS:

Penguin Books have recently issued translations of Herodotus (A. de Selincourt, 1954) and Thucydides (Rex Warner, 1954), and of Homer (E. V. Rieu, *Iliad* 1950, *Odyssey* 1945). These and the other main authors are available in the Loeb series, Greek text with translation opposite.

Two Loeb collections edited by J. M. Edmonds contain the fragments of the poets whose works are lost, and texts relating to their lives: *Lyra Graeca* (vol. I Alcman Arion; II Stesichorus Ibycus Anacreon Lasus Simonides; III Bacchylides, folk-songs, Attic drinking-songs, 1922–7) and *Elegy and Iambus* (vol. I Callinus Tyrtaeus Mimnermus Solon Theognis; II Archilochus, 1931). The Greek text is sometimes adventurous and should be checked against *Diehl, *Anthologia Lyrica* (Teubner, 3rd ed. in progress).

There are also recent translations, with comment, of Plato's *Republic* by F. M. Cornford (1941); Aristotle's *Politics* by Sir E. Barker (1946) and *Constitution of Athens* by von Fritz and Kapp (1950).

*Fragments of lost historians are cited from Jacoby's *Fragmente der griechischen Historiker* (in progress) by the serial number given to each historian and the fragment number, *e.g.* Hippias 6 F 6.

GENERAL HISTORIES:

Cambridge Ancient History, especially vol. III ch. 22, The Dorian States (Prof. H. T. Wade-Gery, 1925) and vol. IV ch. 3, Athens under the Tyrants (Sir F. Adcock, 1926).

Glotz and Cohen, *Histoire grecque*, vol. I (1925).

Bury, *History of Greece* (3rd ed. revised by R. Meiggs, 1951).

GREEK POLITICAL INSTITUTIONS:

Sir A. Zimmern, *The Greek Commonwealth* (5th ed. 1931).

Sir J. Myres, *The Political Ideas of the Greeks* (1927).

T. A. Sinclair, *A History of Greek Political Thought* (1952).

P. N. Ure, *The Origin of Tyranny* (1922), detailed and sometimes forced argument of the thesis that all tyrants were capitalists before they seized power.

M. P. Nilsson, *The Age of the Early Greek Tyrants* (Dill Memorial Lecture, Belfast 1936), tyranny based on the growth of industry and of city population.

Mary White, *Greek Tyranny*, in *Phoenix* 1955, a valuable short survey.

ARCHAEOLOGY AND ART:

G. M. A. Richter, *Archaic Greek Art* (1949).

J. Charbonneaux, *La sculpture grecque archaïque* (1938).

R. J. H. Jenkins, *Dedalica* (1936).

E. Pfuhl, *Masterpieces of Greek Drawing and Painting* (tr. Sir J. Beazley, 1926): there is a larger selection of early material in his unabridged *Malerei und Zeichnung der Griechen*, vol. III (1923).

A. Lane, *Greek Pottery* (1948).

C. T. Seltman, *Greek Coins* (2nd ed. 1955).

D. S. Robertson, *Greek and Roman Architecture* (2nd ed. 1943).

W. B. Dinsmoor, *The Architecture of Ancient Greece* (1950).

Camb. Anc. Hist. plates vols I–II (1927–8).

C. Zervos, *L'Art en Grèce* (1934).

NOTES

(*BSA* = *Annual of the British School at Athens*; *CQ* = *Classical Quarterly*; *JHS* = *Journal of Hellenic Studies*)

CHAPTER I

[1] The political character of Homer's kings is discussed in outline in my lecture *Probouleusis* (Oxford 1954).

[2] Plutarch, *Lycurgus* 6; Her. VI 56–60; Ar. *Pol.* 1285a; Xen. *Const. of Sparta* 15.7 (the oath).

[3] E.g. Ar. *Const. of Athens* 3.

[4] See n. 1.

[5] The script known as Minoan Linear B is now being deciphered as early Greek (M. Ventris and J. Chadwick, *JHS* 1953 84ff., also published separately, and *Antiquity* 1953 196ff.), and we begin to have some exact knowledge of the organisation of Mycenean Greece. This script is a syllabary, quite unrelated to the Phoenician alphabet later adapted for Greek.

[6] Plato, *Rep.* VIII–IX, *Politicus*.

[7] Mainly Ar.*Pol.* 1310b–1315b.

CHAPTER II

[8] Ar. *Pol.* 1285a.

[9] Isocrates, *Philip* 107.

[10] Archilochus fr. 25; *Hippias 6 F 6, *cf.* *Euphorion in Müller, *Fragmenta Historicorum Graecorum* vol. III (1849) p. 72 fr. 1; for Gyges, see Her. I 8–14.

[11] For Solon, see ch. VII; Theognis, *e.g.* 39–60.

[12] *E.g.* Aeschylus, *Choephoroe* 479.

[13] Pindar, *Olympian* I 23, *Pythian* I 60, III 70 (king), III 85 (tyrant); contrast *Pythian* XI 53.

[14] Isocrates, *Euagoras e.g.* 40.

[15] Thuc. II 63.2, 64.5.

[16] Thuc. VI 59.3.

[17] Solon fr. 9; Theognis 52; Isocrates, *Panegyricus* 125–6.

[18] Her. I 59.1, V 78. For his use of *basileus* and *tyrannos*, see Powell, *Lexicon to Herodotus* (1938).

[19] Thuc. I 13.1, 17 (tyrants), VI 54.5 (Peisistratids).

[20] Plato, *Rep. e.g.* IX 587 d–e; Ar. *Pol. e.g.* 1279a; Xen. *Memorabilia* IV 6.12.

[21] Her. III 80–82, *cf.* VI 43.3.

[22] Plato, *Rep.* V 473c. Autocratic power is needed for the conversion of an ordinary to an ideal city (*cf.* VI 502b) but it need not be exercised by a single ruler (VII 540d) nor is the title king necessary ("dynast" V 473d and elsewhere; tyrant, *Laws* IV 709e—Plato's experience in Sicily is relevant here, and the plan to educate Dionysius II, see Plato's seventh letter and Plutarch, *Dion*). But the word king is not confined to this context, *cf. e.g. Rep.* IX 587c.

[23] The discussion which follows V 473c–e is concerned entirely with

the conventional belief that philosophers are politically useless, not with the further paradox I have attributed to Plato in the text: but the latter is clear from the other sources quoted in this chapter.

CHAPTER III

[24] H. L. Lorimer, *BSA* XLII 76ff., with full illustrations.

[25] Archilochus fr. 6; for Tyrtaeus, see Miss Lorimer 121ff.; Callinus fr. 1.5.

[26] Ar. *Pol.* 1297b, *cf.* 1289b.

[27] Mimnermus fr. 14; Strabo 643 (Colophon); *Ar fr. 611.51 (Magnesia).

[28] Her. III 82.4; Plato, *Rep.* VIII 565d; Ar. *Pol.* 1310b.

[29] *Anth. Pal.* XIV 73 (*The Greek Anthology*, Loeb series, tr. Paton, vol. V 1918).

[30] Thuc. I 15.3; Her. V 99; A. Blakeway, *BSA* XXXIII 205f. and *Greek Poetry and Life, Essays presented to Gilbert Murray* (1936) 47ff.; but for the date of Archilochus, F. Jacoby, *CQ* 1941 97ff.

[31] Her. VI 127.3; Ar. *Pol.* 1310b; *Ephorus 70 F 115, 176; Andrewes, *CQ* 1949 70ff.; for coinage, see p. 82 and n. 88.

[32] Mainly Archilochus fr. 3; see Miss Lorimer 115.

[33] Pausanias II 19.2; Andrewes, *CQ* 1951 39ff.

CHAPTER IV

[34] The main sources (not referred to in detail in the following notes) are Her. V 92, III 48–53; *Nicholas of Damascus 90 F 57–60, from Ephorus. See also J. G. O'Neill, *Ancient Corinth* (1930); D. E. W. Wormell, *Hermathena* XLVI (1945) 1ff.; Johansen, *Les vases sicyoniens* (1923: it was then believed that Protocorinthian was made at Sicyon); Payne, *Necrocorinthia* (1931), *Protokorinthische Vasenmalerei* (1933), and the excavation at Perachora published since his death (*Perachora*, vol. I 1940, vol. II in preparation). For sculpture (at Corcyra), Rodenwaldt, *Altdorische Bildwerke in Korfu* (1938).

[35] Thuc. I 13; Dunbabin, *JHS* 1948 59ff.; C. M. Robertson, *JHS* 1940 16–21 (Posideion); for the pottery, see n. 34.

[36] Strabo 378.

[37] *Hicks and Hill, *Greek Historical Inscriptions* (2nd ed. 1901) no. 1. The surviving epitaph is of Roman imperial date, but is probably copied from a much earlier original.

[38] Thuc. I 13.4.

[39] Her. I 14.

[40] Plutarch, *The Oracles at Delphi* 13 400e.

[41] Diodorus VII 9 ; Pausanias II 4.4.

[42] *Nicholas 90 F 35.

[43] Ar. *Pol.* 1305a ; Thuc. I 126.

[44] The ancient evidence for the North-western colonies is scattered : for full references see Busolt, *Griechische Geschichte* (2nd ed. 1893) I 642f.

Calydon : Payne, *Necrocorinthia* 249.

Trebenishte : Filow and Schkorpil, *Die archaische Nekropole von Trebenischte* (1927).

Lyncestis : Strabo 326.

Damastion : J. M. F. May, *The Coinage of Damastion* (1939), 1ff.

[45] Her. V 95.

[46] Theognis 891–4 (like many of the poems in this collection, these lines are certainly not by Theognis himself).

[47] Her. III 48, I 14 (Lydia) ; *Nicholas 90 F 59 (Psammetichus) ; references for Naucratis in R. M. Cook, *JHS* 1937 228.

[48] Ar. *Pol.* 1313a–b.

[49] *Ar. fr. 611.20.

[50] Diogenes Laertius I 94–100. Periander does not appear in the list of Plato, *Protagoras* 343a.

[51] Her. I 23–4 ; Pindar, *Olympian* XIII 16ff.

CHAPTER V

[52] For the Heraclidae etc. see Wade-Gery, *Camb. Anc. Hist.* II (1924) ch. 19. For Doric, C. D. Buck, *Greek Dialects* (3rd. ed. 1955).

[53] *Pollux III 83 ; Plutarch, *Greek Questions* 1.

[54] On the Corinthian tribes, see S. Dow, *Harvard Studies in Classical Philology* 1942 89ff.

[55] Diodorus VIII 24.

[56] *Jacoby 105 F 2.

[57] Ar. *Pol.* 1315b.

[58] Pausanias VI 19. 1–4.

[59] Her. V 67–68 ; *Nicholas 90 F 61 ; Ar. *Pol.* 1316a.

[60] Her. I 67–8 (Orestes) ; Plutarch, *Theseus* 36, *Cimon* 8 (Theseus).

[61] *Scholiast on Pindar, *Nemean* IX. For the Sacred War, Mr. W. G. Forrest has allowed me to make use of an article to be published shortly in *Bulletin de correspondance hellénique* ; the main sources are also given in Ure, *op. cit.* 259ff.

Photographs of Delphi in P. de la Coste Messelière, *Delphes* (1943).

[62] Her. VI 126–30; M. F. McGregor, *Trans. Amer. Phil. Soc.* 1941 266ff.

[63] The ancient evidence is scattered, and different views have been taken of it. The view adopted here is roughly that of Wade-Gery, *Camb. Anc. Hist.* III 543ff.

For Olympia, see Hege and Rodenwaldt, *Olympia* (1936); E. Kunze, *Neue Meisterwerke griechischer Kunst aus Olympia* (1948).

[64] Thuc. IV 41.2; Pindar, *Pythian* V 70.

[65] Pausanias IV 33.2 (Eumelus); Tyrtaeus fr. 11.1.

[66] Thuc. VI 4.6; *cf.* pp. 130–1.

CHAPTER VI

[67] Main sources: Her. I 65–6; Thuc. I 18.1; Plutarch, *Lycurgus*; Ar. *Pol.* 1269a–1271b. The date and nature of the reforms are under continuing dispute: for the seventh century, Wade-Gery, *Camb. Anc. Hist.* III 558ff. and (with detailed discussion of the Rhetra) *CQ* 1943 62ff. and 1944 1ff., 115ff.; for the ninth century, N. G. L. Hammond, *JHS* 1950 42ff. The archaeological evidence is mostly in *Artemis Orthia*, ed. R. M. Dawkins (1929), *cf.* also Tod and Wace, *Catalogue of the Sparta Museum* (1906); on the pottery, E. A. Lane, *BSA* XXXIV 99ff. and B. B. Shefton *BSA* XLIX 299ff.; A. Blakeway, *Classical Review* 1935 185 gives a concise account of the historical implications.

[68] The names occur in a gloss on Her., of which A. Diller publishes an important new text in *American Journal of Philology* 1941 499.

[69] Her. I 65.5; Xen., *Const. of Sparta* 11.

[70] Plutarch, *Lycurgus* 6.

[71] Polybius VI 45.

[72] For Spartan bronze, see the group put together by E. Langlotz, *Frühgriechische Bildhauerschulen* (1927) pl. 44–53, though the attributions are not all equally convincing. The spectacular mixing-bowl found at Vix (R. Joffroy, *Le trésor de Vix*, 1954) appears to be Spartan, and gives an idea of the bowl sent earlier to Croesus (Her. I 70: the present referred to on p. 119).

Many of the ivories (*Artemis Orthia* pl. XCI ff.) show a close relation to Ionian work.

[73] [Plutarch] *Moralia* 238e; *Ar. fr. 611.12.

[74] Ar. *Pol.* 1306b.

[75] Ar. *Pol.* 1271a 36.

[76] Tyrtaeus fr. 1. 12 (Hammond, *op. cit.* 50, takes an entirely different view of this fragment).

[77] *Ar. fr. 541, 540; *cf.* Her. IX 28.2 (Plataea).

[78] Thuc. V 67–8; Xen., *Const. of Sparta* 11.

[79] Tyrtaeus fr. 4.

[80] Plutarch, *Lycurgus* 7, combined with other scattered evidence.

[81] Her. I 65; Plutarch, Lycurgus 1, quoting Simonides and others.

CHAPTER VII

[82] Main sources: Solon (the fragments, which are not numerous, are not cited in detail in the following notes); Ar. *Const. of Athens* 2-13; Plutarch, *Solon*. I. M. Linforth, *Solon the Athenian* (1919); K. Freeman, *The Work and Life of Solon* (1926); W. J. Woodhouse, *Solon the Liberator* (1938); C. Hignett, *A History of the Athenian Constitution* (1952).

[83] *Cf.* V. Desborough, *Protogeometric Pottery* (1952) 296ff.

[84] Western colonisation: T. J. Dunbabin, *The Western Greeks* (1948).

Al Mina: preliminary report, Sir L. Woolley, *JHS* 1938 1ff.; the early Greek pottery, C. M. Robertson *JHS* 1940 2ff.

[85] *E.g.* Theognis 183–92.

[86] Homer, *Iliad* VI 236; Hesiod, *Works and Days* 298ff., 374 and *passim*. *Pollux IX 61 says that fines were reckoned in oxen in Dracon's law-code (p. 84).

[87] The evidence for these iron currencies is scattered and not wholly satisfactory: similar "currencies" are however well known in other areas of the world.

Obols and drachmas: Plutarch, *Lysander* 17; *Ar. fr. 481; the bundle of spits found by the excavators of the Argive Heraeum is illustrated by Ure, *op. cit.* 163, *Camb. Anc. Hist.*, plates vol. I 302, Seltman 35, etc.

[88] The date of the first Greek coinage is generally put too early, see P. Jacobsthal and E. S. G. Robinson, *JHS* 1951 85ff., 156ff.; W. L. Brown, *Numismatic Chronicle* 1950 177ff.

[89] Hesiod, *Works and Days* 686; Alcaeus, Page p. 315 (see n. 97).

[90] Ships on Attic Geometric: G. S. Kirk, *BSA* XLIV 93ff., and for the historical interpretation, 144ff.

Athens and Aegina: Dunbabin, *BSA* XXXVII 83ff.

Protoattic: J. M. Cook, *BSA* XXXV 165ff.; Kübler, *Altattische Malerei* (1950).

[91] Her. V 71; Thuc. I 126–7.

[92] Ar. *Const. of Athens* 4.1, *Pol.* 1274b; Plutarch, *Solon* 17.

[93] Plutarch, *Solon* 8–10.

[94] F. Jacoby, *Atthis* (1949).

[95] The migration had begun before Solon, see Dunbabin, *BSA* XLV 193ff.

[96] Mainly Ar. *Const. of Athens, cf. Pol.* 1273b–1274a.

CHAPTER VIII

[97] The relevant poems of Alcaeus are translated, and the historical situation is fully discussed and documented, in D. L. Page, *Sappho and Alcaeus* (1955). I note below only a few main sources.

[98] Ar. *Pol.* 1311b.

[99] Her. V 94–5.

[100] Strabo 617.

[101] *Lyra Graeca* III p. 532, 26; Ar. *Pol.* 1285a.

[102] Diogenes Laertius I 74–81.

[103] Ar. *Pol.* 1274b.

CHAPTER IX

[104] Main sources: Her. I 59–64 (Peisistratus' rise), V 55–65 (fall of tyranny); Thuc. VI 54–9; Ar. *Const. of Athens* 13–9. For personalities and families, Kirchner, *Prosopographia Attica* (1901–3). Early buildings, I. T. Hill, *The Ancient City of Athens* (1953). Payne and Young, *Archaic Marble Sculpture from the Acropolis* (1936); Langlotz and Schuchhardt, *Archaische Plastik auf der Akropolis* (1943); Sir J. Beazley, *Attic Black-figure, a Sketch* (1928), *Development of Attic Black-figure* (1951), *Panathenaica* in *American Journal of Archaeology* 1943 441ff.; A. Rumpf, *Sakonides* (1937); W. Technau, *Exekias* (1936).

[105] Strabo 392 (Sophocles fr. 24); Thuc. II 55; for Cleisthenes' division see the map in A. W. Gomme, *The Population of Athens in the Fifth and Fourth Centuries B.C.* (1933).

[106] Ar. *Pol.* 1305a.

[107] Her. VI 123–31; Thuc. I 126–7; Plutarch, *Solon* 11.

[108] Her. VI 34–41, 103–4; Wade-Gery, *JHS* 1951 212ff.

[109] *Pherecydes 3 F 2.

[110] Solon fr. 18, 20, 9–10.

[111] Ar. *Pol.* 1314a–1315b.

[112] B. D. Meritt, *Hesperia* 1939 59ff.; T. J. Cadoux, *JHS* 1948 109ff.

[113] See n. 108.

[114] Plutarch, *Solon* 29; *Marmor Parium A 43; Pickard-Cambridge, *The Dramatic Festivals of Athens* (1953) 56.

[115] Mary White (*Phoenix* 1955 17) promises a study of Peisistratid cults and festivals.

[116] Her. V 66, 69ff.; Ar. *Const. of Athens* 20–22.

Chapter X

[117] Herodotus is the main source: I (Croesus and Cyrus), III (Cambyses and Darius), IV (Scythia), V–VI (Ionic Revolt and Marathon), VII–IX (Xerxes' war).

[118] Pindar, *Pythian* I 94; Bacchylides III.

[119] Tartessus: Her. IV 152.

Naucratis: Her. II 178–9; R. M. Cook, *JHS* 1937 227ff.

[120] Her. V 28, I 141–3.

[121] Her. I 163.

[122] Polycrates' rise and sea-power: Her. III 39; *Polyaenus I 23.2; Thuc. I 13. Mary White, *JHS* 1954 36ff., discusses difficulties arising from the attribution of the buildings to Polycrates, and concludes that his father was tyrant before him.

[123] E. Buschor, *Altsamische Standbilder* (1934) pl. 141–3; also illustrated by Ure, *op. cit.* 82; *M. N. Tod, *Greek Historical Inscriptions* (vol. I, 2nd ed. 1946) no. 7.

[124] *Tod, *op. cit.* no. 34.

[125] Her. III 39, 47, I 70; *cf.* n.72.

[126] Sir M. Bowra, *Greek Lyric Poetry* (1936) 260ff.

[127] Her. III 60; for the Heraeum, D. S. Robertson, *op. cit* 95ff., Dinsmoor *op. cit.* 124f., 134ff.

Darius' bridge, Her. IV 87–9.

[128] Bowra, *op. cit.* ch. VI–VII.

[129] Her. III 39.2, 40–3 (Amasis and the ring), 44–5 (Cambyses).

[130] Her. I 69–70, 82–3 (Croesus), 141.4, 152–3 (Ionian appeal).

[131] Her. III 46–7, 54–9.

[132] Her. III 120–8.

[133] Her. III 139–49.

[134] Spartan intervention is attested by Plutarch, *Moralia* 859c-d; the date is disputed, but Diodorus VII 11 suggests 515.

Naxos' power, Her. V 30ff.

[135] Her. IV 136–42.

[136] Her. V 11, 23–4.

[137] Main narrative of the Ionic Revolt: Her. V 28–38, 99–126, VI 1–42. The account of Aristagoras draws on G. de Sanctis, *Problemi di storia antica* (1932) 63ff.

Chapter XI

[138] Main sources: Her. VII 153–62 (Hippocrates and Gelon); Diodorus, the Sicilian chapters in XI (Deinomenids), XII–XVI

(Dionysius etc.). For the detail of sections (a) and (b), see T. J. Dunbabin, *The Western Greeks* (1948 : full discussion down to 480); *Hill, *Sources for Greek History*, B.C. 478–431 (new ed. revised by Meiggs and Andrewes, 1951 : the Greek texts for this period). See also E. A. Freeman, *History of Sicily* (4 vols., 1891–4); the Sicilian chapters in *Camb. Anc. Hist.* IV–VI (1926–7).

[139] Ar. *Pol.* 1310b.

[140] Pindar, *Pythian*, I 95–8 ; Dunbabin 314ff.

[141] Ar. *Pol.* 1316a.

[142] Her. VI 23 ; Thuc. VI 4. 5–6 ; E. S. G. Robinson, *JHS* 1946 13ff.

[143] Ar. *Pol.* 1302b.

[144] Her. V 43–7, VII 158.2.

[145] Pindar, *Pythian* I, *Nemeans* I, IX ; *Oxyrhynchus Papyri* 2257 fr. 1 (Aeschylus).

[146] Hieron : Pindar, *Olympians* I, VI (Agesias), *Pythians* I–III. Theron : *Olympians* II–III.

[147] Ar. *Pol.* 1315b, 1312b.

[148] *Tod, *op. cit.* nos. 17 (Himera), 22 (Cumae : now in the British Museum).

[149] Thuc. VI–VII (reform of the generalship, VI 72).

[150] The remainder of this section is virtually all from Diodorus, who draws on Ephorus (p. 17) and Timaeus (p. 140).

[151] The defences of Euryalus sometimes ascribed to Dionysius (*e.g.* R. G. Collingwood, *Antiquity* 1932 261ff.) are now assigned to Archimedes at a much later date, see A. W. Lawrence, *JHS* 1946 99ff.

[152] Ar. *Pol.* 1305a.

[153] Plutarch, *Dion* and *Timoleon*; Diodorus XVI, XVIII–XX, the Sicilian chapters; Plato, *Letters*, esp. VII and VIII ; and scattered sources.

Chapter XII

[154] H. D. Westlake, *Thessaly in the Fourth Century B.C.* (1935); J. S. Morrison, *CQ* 1942 57ff.

[155] Xen., *Hellenica* VII 1. 44–6, 3.

[156] F. H. Marshall, *The Second Athenian Confederacy* (1905).

[157] W. S. Ferguson, Hellenistic Athens (1911) ch. II–III.

[158] Plutarch, *Aratus* and *Agis and Cleomenes*; F. W. Walbank, *Aratus of Sicyon* (1933); Sir W. Tarn, *Antigonus Gonatas* (1913) 277–86.

INDEX

[Principal entries are in bold type.]

163